IMAGES OF WAR

BRITISH TANKS
THE SECOND WORLD WAR

IMAGES OF WAR

BRITISH TANKS

THE SECOND WORLD WAR

RARE PHOTOGRAPHS FROM WARTIME ARCHIVES

Pat Ware

Pen & Sword
MILITARY

First published in Great Britain in 2011 by
PEN & SWORD MILITARY
an imprint of
Pen & Sword Books Ltd,
47 Church Street,
Barnsley,
South Yorkshire
S70 2AS

A CIP record for this book is available from the British Library.

ISBN 978 1 84884 500 8

Typeset by Chic Media Ltd.

Printed and bound by CPI UK.

Pen & Sword Books Ltd incorporates the Imprints of
Pen & Sword Aviation, Pen & Sword Family History, Pen & Sword
Maritime, Pen & Sword Military, Pen & Sword Discovery, Wharncliffe
Local History, Wharncliffe True Crime, Wharncliffe Transport, Pen &
Sword Select, Pen & Sword Military Classics, Leo Cooper,
The Praetorian Press, Remember When, Seaforth Publishing and
Frontline Publishing.

For a complete list of Pen & Sword titles please contact
Pen & Sword Books Limited
47 Church Street, Barnsley, South Yorkshire, S70 2AS, England
E-mail: enquiries@pen-and-sword.co.uk
Website: www.pen-and-sword.co.uk

Contents

Introduction **6**

Chapter One
The Development of the Tank **9**

Chapter Two
Light Tanks **23**

Chapter Three
Cruiser Tanks **31**

Chapter Four
Infantry Tanks **62**

Chapter Five
Heavy Tanks **85**

Chapter Six
American Tanks in British Service **91**

Chapter Seven
Specials, Engineers' Tanks and 'Funnies' **111**

Introduction

The tank made its first appearance on the Western Front in 1916, but it was to be another two decades before the strategies of tank warfare reached some sort of maturity. By 1939/40, German Blitzkrieg tactics showed what tanks and infantry could achieve in the hands of well-trained commanders who understood their strengths and weaknesses. Although the Wehrmacht *were generally the masters of tank warfare, it is interesting to consider how each of the major combatants approached the question of tank design during this period.*

As you might imagine, the *Wehrmacht* took a rational and organised approach. Between 1939 and 1945, disregarding captured enemy tanks, Germany deployed just six major types of tank, designated *Panzerkampfwagen (PzKpfw) I* to *VI*, with logical modifications and improvements bringing changes in firepower and protection. For example, *PzKpfw I* was a light tank armed with two 7.92mm machine guns, whilst the *PzKpfw II* was equipped with a 20mm gun. The medium *PzKpfw III* of 1937 was the primary weapon of the German Panzer divisions and was armed with a 37mm, and then a 50mm, gun. It remained in production until 1943. The medium-weight *PzKpfw IV* and the heavy/medium *PzKpfw V* Panther, were both armed with a 75mm gun, as was the first variant of the *PzKpfw VI* Tiger. The second iteration of the *PzKpfw VI*, the *Königstiger*, was equipped with the fearsome 88mm gun.

The US Army was possibly even slower off the mark in developing modern tanks than Britain, and in 1939/40, the standard US tanks were the light M1 and M2, and the medium M2. However, for most of the war, production was concentrated on the M3/M5 Stuart light tank and the M4 Sherman medium and, as the war progressed, the US Army preferred to continue to produce large numbers of what were, generally, compromised designs rather than disrupt production in search of perfection.

Although some M2 light tanks came to Britain for training, the type never saw combat and was superseded by the M3/M5 Stuart, armed with a 37mm gun, even before the USA was involved in the conflict. By 1943, the M3/M5 was obsolete and was superseded, in turn, by the M24 Chaffee, which mounted a 75mm gun. The medium M2, also armed with a 37mm gun, quickly gave way to the curious M3 Lee/Grant with both 75mm and 37mm guns, but best known in this class, and the second most numerous tank of the conflict, was the M4 Sherman. Early Shermans mounted a 75mm gun, but this was subsequently replaced by a 76mm weapon; the British also mounted a 17-pounder (76.2mm) gun on the Sherman in a new turret. US heavy tanks included the M6, armed with both 3in and 37mm main guns, but built in very small numbers, and the M26 Pershing, with a 90mm gun, but which came too late in the war to see any action in Europe.

The Soviet Union was similarly slow to respond to the challenges of designing modern tanks and, although the Red Army received Lend-Lease supplies of both British and American tanks, with one notable exception, the Soviet-designed tanks of the period were essentially pre-war designs. The BT series were fast medium tanks based on the designs of the American J. Walter Christie, and was armed with a 37mm, and then a 45mm, main gun; the design dated back to 1935, but the BT-7 remained in production throughout the war. The T-28B medium tank was inspired by British multi-turret machines of the 1930s and was armed with a 76.2mm main gun, but was inadequately armoured. The T-32 and T-35 were heavy tanks, with a 76.2mm main gun, but were unsuccessful due to their sheer size.

The most successful of the Soviet designs was the T-34, which many regard as the best all-round tank design of the war. Armed initially with a 76mm gun but latterly with a more powerful 85mm weapon, the crude, but undeniably effective, T-34 was able to engage the German tanks on a more-or-less equal basis and, with almost 40,000 examples produced, it was the most numerous tank of the conflict.

Having developed the concept of the tank to the point where it had some effect on the outcome of the First World War, you might be forgiven for thinking that Britain would have had the edge in tank design. Sadly, this was not the case! During the early years of the war, British tanks were generally not as well armed nor as well protected as their German counterparts. Rather than concentrating on a small number of designs, and developing these to the point where they were reliable, the British tank factories produced a multiplicity of often outdated and unreliable machines that reflected the questionable strategy of producing separate 'cruiser' and 'infantry' tanks.

Between 1939 and 1945, the British Army had access to some twenty indigenous tank designs, some of them so poor that they were never to see combat, together with Lend-Lease supplies of the American Stuart, Lee/Grant and Sherman tanks. Most numerous of the home-grown tanks was the Valentine, a private venture from Vickers-Armstrongs which accounted for almost one quarter of British tank production during the war years. Others procured in large numbers included the Churchill, the Cromwell and the outdated Matilda. The standard British anti-tank gun in 1939 was the 2-pounder (40mm) and when this proved to be inadequate against the better-armoured German tanks, it was replaced by either the British 6-

pounder (57mm) or the American 75mm gun, both of which packed more punch. However, none of these could compare with the German 75mm and 88mm guns and it was not until 1944, when the Comet was fitted with a 77mm gun, that a British tank could finally face the Germans on a more-or-less equal footing . . . and just 1,186 Comets were constructed, all of them too late for D-Day and the battle for Normandy!

Nevertheless, the British continue to exhibit a love of the underdog and it is our knack of snatching victory from the jaws of defeat, against all the odds, that makes British tank design so fascinating.

Chapter One

The Development of the Tank

Although there had been experiments with armoured traction engines and ammunition road trains during the Boer War, the modern armoured fighting vehicle (AFV) is less than 100 years old. The first design for what could be considered a tank was mooted by a French Army captain in 1903. This was subsequently abandoned, as was a later design produced in Austria. British tanks first saw action in 1916 and, by the end of the First World War, the tank was in service with the armies of Britain, France, Germany, Italy and the USA.

The Birth of the Tank

From around the turn of the century, experiments had been conducted into the feasibility of producing iron-clad 'landships' which could mount a large-calibre gun and which would be sufficiently well-protected to be able to operate under fire on the battlefield. Improvised armoured cars started to appear during the early stages of the First World War, when boilerplate was used to provide a measure of protection against small arms and machine-gun fire, but their usefulness was severely restricted by a lack of mobility.

As First Lord of the Admiralty, Winston Churchill established what was known as the 'Landship Committee' to investigate the possibility of developing a cross-country armoured vehicle. A specification was drawn up by Lieutenant-Colonel Ernest D. Swinton in October 1914 and there were experiments with wheeled vehicles. However, it was the continuous caterpillar crawler track devised by the American Benjamin Holt in 1907 that suggested a way forward.

The first workable prototype for a tracked armoured vehicle was produced in Britain when, in September 1915, William Foster & Company, agricultural engineers based in Lincoln, constructed what became known as 'Little Willie'. Designed by William Tritton and Lieutenant Walter G. Wilson, by the beginning of 1916 Little Willie had been followed by a second prototype, known as 'Mother' or 'Big Willie'. This machine was sufficiently successful that Fosters were contracted to build an initial twenty-five units, with contributions towards a further 150 also coming from the Metropolitan Amalgamated Railway Carriage and Wagon Company. Described as the 'tank, Mk I', these early machines consisted of a huge rhomboidal box-like hull of riveted boilerplate, with unsprung steel tracks wrapped around the perimeter. For reasons of security, the machines were initially described as 'water carriers for Mesopotamia' – thus giving rise to the name 'tank' – and were assigned to a new unit known as the Heavy Section, Machine Gun Corps. The design of the tank evolved rapidly and, by 1917, the Mk VIII was being constructed to a standardised design in both Britain and the USA.

'Medium' tanks started to appear at the beginning of 1917, against a War Office requirement for a lighter, faster machine. The first of these, the twin-engined medium Mk A (or Whippet), was designed by William Tritton and William Rigby, and went into action in March 1918. The Mk B was designed by Walter G. Wilson, by now a Major, and incorporated elements of both the original Mk I and the Whippet. This was followed by the Mk C, or Hornet, of 1917, of which some 200 examples were constructed, the type remaining in British service until about 1923.

Whilst it was the British Army which fielded the first tanks, the Germans were quick to copy a captured Whippet and their Leicht *Kampwagen* (Lk II) was prototyped in 1918, and the first production example of the huge *Sturmpanzerwagen A7V* appeared in October 1917. Similarly, the French produced their first tanks, in the form of the Schneider *Char d'Assaut 1 (CA 1)* and the *Char St Chamond* during 1916. However, the most significant French tank design of the First World War was the Renault *Char Canon FT-1*, the first tank to incorporate a revolving turret, with a 37mm gun, and track suspension. This design was also adopted by the US Army as the M1917.

The Interwar Period

With the exception of a few half-finished medium Mk Cs, tank production in Britain came to a halt following the signing of the Armistice in November 1917. Many existing heavy and medium tanks remained in service, but outstanding production contracts were cancelled. However, despite considerable scepticism, there were those who believed that the tank was here to stay and development of the faster medium Mk D was continued, whilst work was also initiated on a series of advanced light infantry tanks. Both were designed by Lieutenant-Colonel Philip Johnson of the newly created Tank Design Department, but it was not long before both projects were in trouble. The medium Mk D was cramped and inadequately armed, and there were difficulties with its tensioned wire-rope suspension system and cable tracks. Only four examples were constructed. Johnson's light infantry tank appeared in November 1921 but, despite the prototype acquitting itself well in trials, it did not go into production. Rival designs for the latter role were produced by Vickers-

Armstrongs in 1921, but these lacked speed and reliability, and the transmission was particularly prone to problems.

By 1922/23, Vickers had produced a new design which was designated light tank Mk I – later known as the 'Vickers medium' when lighter designs appeared. Powered by an eight-cylinder air-cooled engine, it was fast and manoeuvrable, and featured a 3-pounder (47mm) gun in a rotating turret. Replacing the earlier Mk C, it was the first British tank to enter service after the First World War.

In 1928/29, attempts were made to improve the design, with the experimental A6 medium Mk III; this was followed by a further three experimental vehicles, designated A7. The failure of the A6 and A7 projects led to some fresh thinking about the role of the tank and when the prototype A9 appeared in 1936 it was described as cruiser tank Mk I. Designed by Sir John Carden of Vickers-Armstrongs as a replacement for the A6 medium Mk III, this was the first British tank to have a powered turret. Production started in 1937, with some 125 vehicles built, and the type remained in service until the end of 1941.

Years earlier, Carden-Loyd (Carden's previous company) had been busy designing a series of one-man tanks – or tankettes – some 325 of which were procured for the British Army. When Carden-Loyd was taken over by Vickers in 1928, the design evolved into the Vickers light tank. The first of these was known as the Carden-Loyd Mk VII, but it was the subsequent two-man Mk VIII that entered service in Britain in 1929. Designated light tank Mk I, the design incorporated Horstman leaf-spring suspension, and was armed with a .303in machine gun in a rotating turret. A programme of gradual improvement led to the Mks IA, II, IIA, IIB, III, IV and V, before the much-improved Mk VI appeared in 1936 with room for a crew of three, and a redesigned turret. Further developments resulted in the Mks VIA, VIB and VIC, which saw service in northern France in 1940.

Light tanks of the Second World War included the Mk VII Tetrarch, and the Mk VIII Harry Hopkins, both of which were considered to be suitable for airborne operations.

British Tank Nomenclature

When the first tanks had appeared in 1916, they were described simply as 'tank Mk I'. Subsequent models were identified as Mk II, Mk III, etc., with minor modifications indicated by a star (e.g. Mk V***). The appearance of the lighter tank in 1917, typified by the Whippet, saw the originals described as heavy tanks, and the smaller machines described as medium tanks. The new Vickers medium tanks which entered service in 1923 were described as light tanks in order to differentiate them from the wartime medium tanks but, just to add to the confusion, were subsequently reclassified as medium tanks when smaller light tanks were introduced in 1930.

From 1926, prototypes of tanks produced for the War Office were allocated 'A' numbers, with individual examples identified by an 'E' suffix and a number (e.g. A6E1). It was not until 1940 that British tanks were also given names, together with a second series of numbers to indicate modifications. A typical description was, thus, 'tank, infantry, Mk IV, Churchill II'.

Infantry and Cruiser Tanks

By 1938, British military thinking held that tanks were intended either for the independent mobile role – in which case they were referred to as cruiser tanks, reflecting naval practice that described large warships as cruisers – or were intended for infantry support, being described as infantry tanks. Field-Marshal Montgomery proposed abandoning this distinction in July 1944, but the concept of infantry and cruiser tanks survived until just after the Second World War when, for a short while, the description of choice was capital tank, this eventually giving way to the now-familiar main battle tank (MBT).

The Emergence of British Specialised Armour Units

The British Army's Machine Gun Corps (MGC) had been formed in October 1915 in an attempt to co-ordinate response to the proliferation of machine guns on the Western Front. In a deliberate attempt to avoid revealing what was felt to be a new 'wonder weapon', the first tanks were operated by six companies of the Heavy Section of the Machine Gun Corps, formed in March 1916 expressly for this purpose. The name was changed to the Heavy Branch in November of that year, by which time there were eight companies, each expanded to form battalions, lettered 'A' through 'H'. In July 1917, the Heavy Branch was separated from the Machine Gun Corps to become the Tank Corps, with seven more battalions, lettered 'I' through 'O', in existence by January 1918, when they all were converted to numbered units. By December 1918, the Tank Corps consisted of twenty-six battalions; twenty-five of these deployed tanks, the remaining unit being assigned to armoured cars.

After the Armistice, the Tank Corps was reduced in size to a central depot and the 2nd, 3rd, 4th and 5th Battalions. In 1920, twelve armoured car companies were established as part of the Tank Corps, absorbing units from the Machine Gun Corps. Eight of these were subsequently converted into independent light tank companies, but all had been disbanded by 1939. On 18 October 1923, the Tank Corps became the Royal Tank Corps and, in April 1939, the Royal Armoured Corps (RAC) was created by combining the Royal Tank Corps – which was renamed the Royal Tank Regiment (RTR) – with the now-mechanised cavalry units. The Reconnaissance Corps was absorbed into the RAC in 1944. At the outbreak of war, the RTR consisted of eight regular battalions, numbered 1 through 8, plus a large number of territorial battalions, and what were described as 'hostilities-only' battalions. The regiment was further expanded during the war.

Mention should also be made of the Experimental Mechanized Force (EMF), a brigade-sized formation under the command of Colonel R. J. Collins, which was intended to investigate and develop the techniques and equipment required for armoured warfare. Established on 27 August 1927 and renamed the Experimental Armoured Force (EAF) the following year, it participated in exercises designed to pit mechanised forces – mounted in armoured cars, Carden-Loyd tankettes and Vickers medium tanks, and supported by machine guns and artillery – against traditionally organised and trained infantry and cavalry. The force was disbanded in 1929.

British Tanks in 1939

By 1938, mechanisation of the British Army was proceeding rapidly, with light tanks being favoured since they were relatively cheap, easy to maintain and ideal for training. When war was declared the following year, the Royal Armoured Corps had around 1,100 tanks available, 90 per cent of which were light tank Mk VIs, armed with nothing more than a pair of machine guns, and really only suitable for reconnaissance duties. There were also sixty-seven Matilda infantry tanks Mks I and II, the former also armed with machine guns, and seventy-nine examples of the more modern cruiser tanks Mks I to IV. The infantry tank Mk II and the cruisers were armed with the Royal Ordnance Factory (ROF) quick-firing (QF) 2-pounder (40mm) armour-piercing gun. This had been designated the standard anti-tank weapon back in October 1934, but was scarcely adequate against the German armour of 1939/40.

The British Expeditionary Force (BEF) took this ragbag collection of machinery to France in 1940, facing a total of 3,380 German tanks. When the BEF was forced to evacuate from Dunkirk, all but thirteen of the 500 tanks that had been shipped to France were abandoned. The experiences gained in France made it obvious that the light tank was obsolete, and it was abandoned soon after. Similarly, the 2-pounder (40mm) gun proved to be insufficiently powerful and whilst later British tanks were equipped with either the British 6-pounder (57mm) or the American 75mm gun, it was not until 1944 that the British finally received tanks which could face the German Tigers on a more equal footing.

However, in 1940 it was obvious that Britain desperately needed a new design of tank – one that would be fast, well protected and sufficiently well armed to take on the Germans. Unfortunately, there was no time to develop such a machine properly. Most of the British designs that were introduced during the next two or three years suffered from mechanical and design faults that could have been avoided if more time had been spent on development, and Britain struggled throughout the war with a multiplicity of designs, often unsatisfactory.

Tanks first saw action at Flers-Courcelette on 15 September 1916 and, although few of the forty-nine vehicles deployed were able to reach their objective, the army Chiefs of Staff were sufficiently impressed with their performance to order more machines. *(Warehouse Collection)*

In March 1917, five Mk II tanks were used as development 'mules' to try out various transmission systems. The engine of the tank shown here drives the tracks through a Williams-Janney hydraulic system, using pumps with adjustable swash plates to alter the speed. The Model T radiator, together with a pair of radiators from Daimler motor cars, was installed in an attempt at keeping the transmission oil at a reasonable temperature. *(Warehouse Collection)*

Whilst the Mk I required a crew of eight men – commander, driver, four gunners and two steersmen, the Mk V, seen here at the Tank Museum, was the first of the series that could be controlled by one man. Nevertheless, conditions inside the hull were intolerable. *(Warehouse Collection)*

Timber decoy or camouflage version of the Mk V tank. *(Warehouse Collection)*

Gun mounts were provided on either side of the early tanks, with the so-called 'male' variants (seen here) equipped with 6-pounders (57mm), and 'females' armed with Hotchkiss machine guns. The tanks were easily defeated by wide trenches. *(Warehouse Collection)*

The Mk V* and Mk V** were three feet longer than the Mk IV in order to improve trench-crossing performance. The US Army also deployed British-built tanks and this photograph was taken at the Tank Corps School in Raleigh, North Carolina. *(US National Archives)*

It can be argued that it was actually the French who came up with the tank in the form that we would recognise it today, in the shape of the Renault FT-17. *(Warehouse Collection)*

Some 1,600 examples of the Renault FT-17 remained in service with the French Army until at least 1939, with some of these pressed into German service, as the *PzKpfw.18R 730(f)*, when France fell in 1940. *(Warehouse Collection)*

By 1922/23, Vickers had produced a new design, initially designated light tank Mk I, but later universally known as the 'Vickers medium' when lighter designs appeared. *(Warehouse Collection)*

The Vickers medium was developed through Mks I, II and IIA and provided the backbone of the Royal Tank Corps during the interwar period. Around 160 examples were constructed, both by Vickers and the Royal Ordnance Factory (Woolwich) over a five-year period. This is the Mk II. *(Warehouse Collection)*

All variants of the Vickers medium were armed with a 3-pounder (47mm) gun together with Hotchkiss or Vickers machine guns. This is a Mk II* from 1926. *(Tank Museum)*

Typified by this Mk II*, the Vickers medium was the first British tank to feature a rotating turret. Some remained in service for training into the early years of the Second World War. *(Tank Museum)*

Just three examples were built of the improved A6 medium tank Mk III in 1930/31. There was no series production. *(Warehouse Collection)*

Armed with a 3-pounder (47mm) main gun and five Vickers machine guns, the medium Mk III was often described as the 'sixteen tonner'. *(Warehouse Collection)*

The A6 was followed by a further three experimental vehicles, designated A7 and designed to be built at the Royal Ordnance Factory (Woolwich). *(Warehouse Collection)*

The experimental A14, dating from 1938, was the first attempt at building a heavy cruiser tank. It was intended to be fitted with a 2-pounder (40mm) gun in the turret, together with a pair of Besa machine guns in small auxiliary turrets, but was never completed. *(Warehouse Collection)*

Experiments with buoyancy compartments during the 1930s led to the development of this Vickers A4 amphibious light tank. The work proved to be something of a dead end, and when amphibious tanks were used in the D-Day landings, flotation screens were used in place of the buoyancy compartments. *(Warehouse Collection)*

Chapter Two

Light Tanks

The British light tank was derived from the Carden-Loyd one-man tanks, or tankettes, dating from 1926. The Mk VI was effectively the final iteration of the original series although, in reality, it was obsolete even before entering service. Following the withdrawal from France in 1940, many of the Mk VI tanks that remained in service were reserved for training duties, although the type also saw some service in Greece and North Africa in 1941.

The much-improved light tank Mk VII, also known as the Tetrarch, was put into production between 1940 and 1942 and actually saw action on D-Day, whilst the later Mk VIII, or Harry Hopkins, was manufactured between 1942 and 1944. Both were built in small numbers by the now-renamed Metropolitan-Cammell Carriage and Wagon Company, which had been a part-owned subsidiary of Vickers-Armstrongs since 1919. Although no match for German armour of the period, both were considered suitable for the support of airborne operations, albeit that the Harry Hopkins was never used in anger.

No new light tanks were considered for production after 1944 – although it is worth pointing out that the aluminium-armoured Alvis CVR(T) (combat vehicle, reconnaissance, tracked), development of which started in 1960, is often described as a light tank.

Light Tank Mk VI
Produced by Vickers-Armstrongs, the three-man light tank Mk VI entered service in 1936, with production continuing until 1940. It was similar in design to the earlier Mk V, with a maximum 14mm riveted hull, but with the turret redesigned to provide space for a Number 7 radio set. Power came from a Meadows ESTL or ESTB six-cylinder engine producing 88bhp, mounted alongside the driver and driving through a five-speed Vickers-Meadows manual gearbox to the front sprockets. There were malleable cast-iron tracks supported on four rubber-tyred road wheels, mounted in pairs on bell cranks with double-spring Vickers-Horstman suspension units. These suspension units, which had appeared on most of the Vickers light tanks up to Mk VI, had been designed by Sydney Horstman, the son of a German watchmaker who had settled in Bath in 1854, changing his name from Horstmann after the end of the First World War.

With a length of just 155in and an overall width of 81in, the 5.2-ton machine was extremely compact, and was capable of a top speed of 30mph on improved surfaces, and 25mph across country, with a range of 130 miles.

The main armament was a Vickers 0.5in machine gun, and there was a co-axial .303in water-cooled machine gun, together with a .303in Bren gun for anti-aircraft defence. Purpose-built anti-aircraft variants had a power-operated turret carrying a bank of four 7.92mm Besa air-cooled machine guns.

On the Mk VIA, the circular commander's cupola was replaced by an octagonal design with two vision slots. The Mk VIB was similar, but reverted to the circular cupola and was simplified in various ways to aid production; it was also produced in the so-called 'India pattern', without the cupola but with a commander's periscope. The Mk VIC omitted the commander's cupola altogether and incorporated co-axial 15mm and 7.92mm Besa machine guns in place of the Vickers guns of the earlier versions; the track width was increased and the engine was also upgraded to increase the top speed to 35mph.

Following their withdrawal from combat, a number of Mk VI light tanks were converted to forward observation posts and some were garrisoned on the island of Malta. The type was also widely used for training.

Light Tank Mk VII (A17) – Tetrarch

Designed by Vickers-Armstrongs as a speculative venture in 1937, the light tank Mk VII was shown to the army in 1938 as a possible cavalry tank. Initially known as Purdah, but eventually dubbed Tetrarch, it was approved for further development as a possible reconnaissance vehicle. This took rather longer than had been anticipated and it was not until July 1940 that a finished prototype was supplied for trials, with the first production example delivered in November 1940.

The three-man vehicle had a completely new hull design – still of riveted construction, but larger and with a maximum armour thickness of 16mm, it measured 162in in length, with a width of 81in. Power came from a horizontally-opposed twelve-cylinder Meadows Type 30 engine producing 165bhp, driving the rear sprockets through a five-speed gearbox. There was also improved suspension using the long-travel Christie system which combined swinging arms with long coil springs. The tracks were carried on four equal-sized road wheels, which also served as track-return rollers. Despite the weight increasing to 7.6 tons, it was capable of a top speed of almost 40mph on the road, and 25mph across country.

However, perhaps the most significant change was the use of a larger main gun – a Vickers 2-pounder (40mm) weapon was fitted to the prototype in place of the 0.5in machine gun used on previous light tanks; some vehicles were equipped with a Littlejohn adaptor which provided a squeeze-bore effect. There was also a co-axial machine gun and a .303in Bren gun for anti-aircraft use. The close-support variant (light tank Mk VII CS) was fitted with a 3in howitzer.

At least one Tetrarch was fitted experimentally with a wading screen and Straussler duplex-drive, allowing amphibious operation. Successful trials of this system on the Tetrarch led to its adaptation for Valentine and Sherman tanks.

A total of 177 examples were constructed during 1941/42, and a number were used during the invasion of Madagascar in 1942. Some were supplied to the Soviet Union where they saw action in 1942. The remainder were put into reserve, and the small size and relatively low weight of the Tetrarch made it suitable for airborne operations, with six or so vehicles carried in a modified version of the Hamilcar glider during the invasion of Normandy in 1944. A number were also deployed during the crossing of the River Rhine in spring 1945 and, surprisingly, the type remained in service until 1949.

Light Tank Mk VIII (A25) – Harry Hopkins

Prototyped during 1941, the light tank Mk VIII – or Harry Hopkins – was the last of the British light tanks, and was a logical development of the Tetrarch. The length of the hull, which now incorporated both riveted and welded elements, was increased to 168in, and the width to 107in, whilst the frontal armour was redesigned and increased in thickness to 38mm. The turret was also redesigned to improve its ballistic performance. These changes increased the weight to 8.5 tons and, retaining the twelve-cylinder Meadows Type 30 engine of the Tetrarch, the maximum speed on the road was reduced to 30mph. The five-speed transmission and the warp/manual steering systems were also carried over from the Tetrarch, although hydraulic assistance was provided for the steering systems, which had previously required considerable physical effort. Testing of early production machines revealed weaknesses in the suspension, possibly due to the increase in weight, and this led to some delays in production while a solution was found.

As with the Tetrarch, the main gun was the 2-pounder (40mm), which in some cases was also fitted with the Littlejohn adaptor to increase muzzle velocity. There was also a co-axial 7.92mm Besa machine gun.

By the time the Harry Hopkins went into production it was effectively obsolete and, with the airborne role assigned to the Tetrarch, none saw any action. A number were handed over to the RAF as airfield defence vehicles and, in 1945, a small number of Alectos, a self-propelled gun variant of the Harry Hopkins, were converted to tank 'dozers for the Royal Engineers, with a hydraulically-operated blade fitted in place of the gun.

Production was once again entrusted to the Vickers-owned Metropolitan-Cammell Carriage and Wagon Company, with a total of ninety-nine vehicles constructed between 1942 and 1944, against an initial anticipated requirement of 1,000.

Production of the light tank Mk VI ended in 1940, by which time around 1,700 units had been constructed. Continued development led to the production of the Mks VIA, VIB and VIC, of which the Mk VIB was the most numerous. The Mk VI saw action in France in 1940, and was deployed in Libya, Greece, Iran/Iraq (Persia) and Egypt, but was easily out-gunned by heavier German and Italian tanks; there were also anti-aircraft variants based on the MK VIA and VIB chassis. *(Warehouse Collection)*

Dating from 1932, the A4 light tank Mk IV was used for training in the early years of the Second World War. This example is fitted with the so-called 'India pattern' turret with a cupola. *(Warehouse Collection)*

The track-return roller of the light tank Mk VIA was moved from the front bogie unit and mounted on the hull side between the two bogies, whilst the circular commander's cupola was replaced by an octagonal design with two vision slots. *(Warehouse Collection)*

The British Army did not purchase any purpose-built tank transporters until 1938/39 and tanks were carried on flat-bed trucks or trailers. This is another Mk VIA light tank, with the octagonal commander's cupola. *(Warehouse Collection)*

The light tank Mk VII – better known as Tetrarch after the Greek word for a ruler – was an unusual machine, much improved on previous light tank designs. Although there was no immediate need for the machine, a production contract was placed, with initial production taking place at Vickers' Elswick factory near Newcastle, before being transferred to the Metropolitan-Cammell Carriage and Wagon Company's works. The Tetrarch was the only airborne tank to see action during the war. *(Warehouse Collection)*

48

Steering the Tetrarch was achieved by turning all four of the armoured-steel road wheels, effectively warping the tracks; tight turns and turns made at low speeds were accommodated by the use of manual track brakes, thus inducing skid turns. *(Warehouse Collection)*

Rear stowage sketch for the Tetrarch light tank Mk VII. *(Warehouse Collection)*

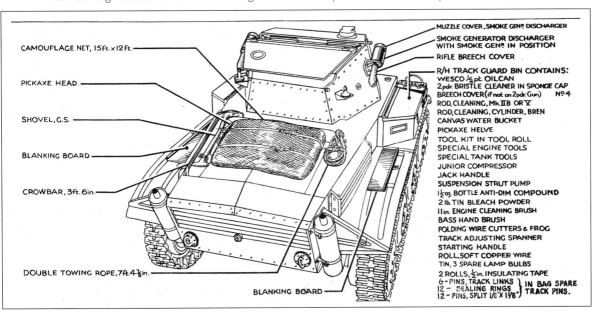

CAMOUFLAGE NET, 15 ft. x 12 ft.

PICKAXE HEAD

SHOVEL, G.S.

BLANKING BOARD

CROWBAR, 3 ft. 6 in.

DOUBLE TOWING ROPE, 7 ft. 4⅝ in.

BLANKING BOARD

MUZZLE COVER, SMOKE GENᴿ DISCHARGER

SMOKE GENERATOR DISCHARGER WITH SMOKE GENᴿ IN POSITION

RIFLE BREECH COVER

R/H TRACK GUARD BIN CONTAINS:
WESCO ½ pt. OILCAN
2 pdr. BRISTLE CLEANER IN SPONGE CAP
BREECH COVER (if not on 2pdr Gun)   Nº 4
ROD, CLEANING, Mk.IIB OR V
ROD, CLEANING, CYLINDER, BREN
CANVAS WATER BUCKET
PICKAXE HELVE
TOOL KIT IN TOOL ROLL
SPECIAL ENGINE TOOLS
SPECIAL TANK TOOLS
JUNIOR COMPRESSOR
JACK HANDLE
SUSPENSION STRUT PUMP
1½ oz. BOTTLE ANTI-DIM COMPOUND
2 lb. TIN BLEACH POWDER
11 in. ENGINE CLEANING BRUSH
BASS HAND BRUSH
FOLDING WIRE CUTTERS & FROG
TRACK ADJUSTING SPANNER
STARTING HANDLE
ROLL, SOFT COPPER WIRE
TIN, 3 SPARE LAMP BULBS
2 ROLLS, ½ in. INSULATING TAPE
6 - PINS, TRACK LINKS
12 -   SEALING RINGS   } IN BAG SPARE
12 - PINS, SPLIT 1/8 X 1⅛)   TRACK PINS.

The Harry Hopkins (light tank Mk VIII) was named after one of Franklin D. Roosevelt's closest advisors, who was unofficial emissary to Winston Churchill. By the time it went into production it was effectively obsolete – in a bold, but ultimately futile, gesture a Harry Hopkins tank was selected for trials as part of the Carrier Wing project. This proposed that light tanks could be fitted with wings and launched from transport aircraft in support of parachute and glider-borne troops – the plan was abandoned when the prototype crashed after take-off. *(Warehouse Collection)*

The Harry Hopkins chassis was adapted to provide the basis for the Alecto self-propelled gun, which mounted a 95mm howitzer low in the hull, and was intended to provide close support for airborne troops. A few of these were operated by armoured car regiments in the immediate post-war years. In the same way, later versions, Alecto III and IV, were planned to be fitted with 25- (88mm) or 32-pounder (159mm) guns respectively, but none were actually constructed. *(Warehouse Collection)*

Chapter Three

Cruiser Tanks

The cruiser tank – sometimes called the 'cavalry tank' – was seen as a medium-weight, fast machine which could make reconnaissance forays deep into enemy territory, much as horse-mounted cavalry had in former conflicts.

Modern thinking on tank design demands that equal attention be paid to mobility, firepower and protection. These principles were not as well accepted in the mid-1930s when the concept of the cruiser tank was first mooted and the emphasis on the speed of the cruiser tank was generally at the expense of armoured protection and firepower – for the first years of the war, British cruisers were armed only with a 2-pounder (40mm) anti-tank gun.

As the Second World War progressed, the role of the cruiser tank, as originally envisaged, became less and less clear and battlefield experience showed that the cruisers were vulnerable to more powerful German anti-tank weapons – the fearsome 88mm *KwK L/56* gun of the Tiger being an extreme case in point. The 2-pounder (40mm) gun was soon replaced by a 6-pounder (57mm) and then, in some cases, by 75mm, 77mm and 17-pounder (76.2mm) guns in an effort to engage German armour on equal terms. Of these, probably only the 17-pounder (76.2mm) and the related 77mm were superior to the German 88mm, particularly when firing armour-piercing discarding sabot (APDS) rounds.

Eleven cruiser tank designs were produced between 1934 and 1945. Some never saw enemy action at all and were retained for training purposes; others saw action but were no match for the German machines. Only two of the designs were really satisfactory – the Meteor-engined Cromwell and the up-gunned Comet variant.

Cruiser Tank Mk I (A9)

What became known as the A9 cruiser tank Mk I was originally conceived as a medium tank to replace the Vickers A6 medium tanks Mks I and II. Development work had started in 1934 under the direction of Sir John Carden of Vickers-Armstrongs, with a view to coming up with a cheaper and more effective design. The A9 was notable for being the first British tank to incorporate a ballistically designed hull, albeit that the maximum thickness of armour was not sufficient and the machine-gun turrets were vulnerable. It was also the first to be fitted with a centrally positioned hydraulically powered turret, and was the first to incorporate the Vickers-Gerlach tank periscope, rather than using direct-vision heavy glass blocks. The A9 was also a pioneer in deep wading and, in 1939, one example was successfully driven completely submerged.

The tank was relatively small: the low hull had a length of just 231in and a width of 100in. Riveted construction was used throughout, with a maximum thickness of armour of 14mm, giving a combat weight of around 12 tons. There was no separation of the driving and fighting compartments and the hull must have been a tight fit for the standard six-man crew. Vickers had proposed that a Rolls-Royce Phantom II engine be used, but production vehicles were powered by a rear-mounted AEC A179 six-cylinder petrol engine, producing 150bhp from 9,630cc, and driving the rear sprockets through a five-speed manual gearbox. Utilising the Vickers 'slow motion' suspension, the road wheels were arranged in threes on a pair of bogies, the front and rear wheels on each side being of larger diameter. A large single spring was provided for each bogie, together with a Newton and Bennett telescopic hydraulic shock absorber. Top speed was in the order of 25mph on the road and 15mph across country, with a range of 100–145 miles.

For the prototype, the main gun was a 3-pounder (47mm) but all production vehicles were armed with the standard 2-pounder (40mm), together with three Vickers .303in water-cooled machine guns: one coaxial with the main gun, the other two in auxiliary turrets on either side of the hull. A fan was fitted in the hull to clear the gun fumes. There was also a close-support variant – cruiser tank Mk I CS – which mounted a 3.7in howitzer in place of the standard 2-pounder (40mm) gun.

A total of just 125 vehicles were constructed: fifty by Vickers-Armstrongs and sevnty-five by Harland and Wolff in Belfast. The Mk I cruisers saw service in France in 1940 and in the Middle East the following year; however, although the main gun was effective against the Italian tanks, it was no match for the more sophisticated German machines. The crews also complained that the design was unreliable and was prone to shedding tracks.

Cruiser Tank Mk II (A10)

Three months after starting work on the A9, Sir John Carden's team at Vickers-Armstrongs began designing an infantry version, designated A10. However, despite the armour being increased to a maximum of 30mm using bolt-on plates, the design was felt to be inadequately protected for the infantry-support role and it was reclassified as a heavy cruiser, becoming the cruiser tank Mk II. Even as a cruiser it was not successful, however, and despite the suspension being found to work well in the desert, the War Office criticised the machine for being slow and underpowered, with a poor cross-country performance.

In design the hull was similar to the A9, although the auxiliary machine-gun turrets were omitted, which allowed the crew to be reduced to five. The Vickers 'slow motion' suspension was retained, as was the AEC A179 petrol engine and the five-speed transmission. Measuring 217in in length, making it slightly shorter than the A9, but with the width identical at 100in, the additional armour put the weight up to 13.75 tons, having the effect of bringing the top speed down to 16mph on hard surfaces and 8mph off the road.

The main gun was the 2-pounder (40mm); there was also a single coaxial Vickers .303in water-cooled machine gun, and a 7.92mm Besa machine gun in a barbette to the right of the hull, making it the first British tank to be fitted with an air-cooled machine gun. On the Mk IIA there was an armoured radio housing and a redesigned mount for the main gun; the Vickers machine gun was also omitted in favour of a second 7.92mm Besa machine gun. As with the A9, there was also a close-support variant (cruiser tank Mk II CS) mounting a 3.7in howitzer.

Production started in 1938, and the type was built by Vickers-Armstrongs (ten), Metropolitan-Cammell Carriage and Wagon Company (forty-five) and the Birmingham Railway Carriage and Wagon Company (120). Like the A9, the A10 was never considered to be more than a stop-gap measure whilst the A13 was developed.

Cruiser Tank Mk III (A13)

The cruiser tank Mk III was probably the most significant British tank of the interwar period and made much of what had gone before redundant. Developed by Morris Commercial Cars and constructed in small numbers by the company's newly established munitions subsidiary, Nuffield Mechanizations and Aero, it was the first British tank to incorporate the suspension that had been designed by the American J. Walter Christie. Using a combination of short swinging arms bearing against long coil springs, the suspension gave the tank a standard of off-road performance that was far in advance of anything previously seen in a British tank and the Christie suspension went on to be used on all subsequent British cruiser tanks.

Although Morris Commercial had been supplied with two Christie tanks from the USA during 1936, the hull of these machines was considered to be too small to accept the typical British turret and the decision was made to incorporate the suspension into a completely new hull. The opportunity was also taken to incorporate Newton and Bennett telescopic hydraulic shock absorbers. The A13 was powered by a rear-mounted Nuffield Liberty V12 tank engine, the origins of which went back to an aero engine designed in 1917. With a power output of 340bhp from a capacity of 27,022cc, the engine was coupled to the rear sprockets via a four-speed manual gearbox. In prototype form, the vehicle was capable of a maximum speed on the road of more than 35mph, with 25mph achievable across country – this led to various mechanical problems. Eventually the road speed was governed to 30mph; in conjunction, the transmission was modified and the tracks redesigned, with a shorter pitch between links.

With an overall height of 100in, and an overall length of 237in, the A13 seemed long and low, an illusion reinforced by the large-diameter road wheels that also served as track-return rollers. The turret was similar to that fitted to the A9 and A10, and the main gun was the familiar 2-pounder (40mm), together with a coaxial Vickers .303in water-cooled machine gun. The maximum thickness of armour was just 14mm, giving a battle weight of 14 tons.

Trials began in October 1937; in January 1938, even before the trials were completed, sixty-five vehicles were ordered, with deliveries scheduled to begin in early 1939.

Cruiser Tank Mk IV (A13 Mk II)

With the design redesignated as A13 Mk II, the cruiser tank Mk IV was fitted with a new style of turret that incorporated distinctive V-section side plates to give a spaced armour configuration. At the same time, new minimum requirements for the armoured protection of cruiser tanks resulted in the maximum thickness of armour on the hull being increased to 30mm, raising the total weight of the vehicle to 14.75 tons. Some examples were built with additional armour covering the gun mantlet. Whilst the turret may have been redesigned, the main gun was still the 2-pounder (40mm), and there was also a coaxial Vickers .303in water-cooled machine gun, which, on the Mk IVA, was replaced by a Besa 7.92mm machine gun. A close-support variant was also produced, mounting a 3.7in howitzer and designated cruiser tank Mk IV CS. The engine, transmission and running gear were unchanged and, despite the increase in overall weight, the maximum road speed remained 30mph.

Some sources suggest that the total production amounted to 655 vehicles, of which 455 were produced by Nuffield Mechanizations and Aero, and a further 200 by the London Midland and Scottish Railway (LMS) workshops, English Electric and Leyland; others suggest that the figure was 240. The A13 Mk II was withdrawn from active service at the end of 1941, but remained in use as a training vehicle.

Cruiser Tank Mk V (A13 Mk III) – Covenanter

In June 1937, two new designs of cruiser tank were planned – the A14, which was to be powered by a Thornycroft marine engine, and the A16, which was to be fitted with the Nuffield Liberty engine. A prototype for the A14 was constructed before both designs were then cancelled and replaced by the lighter and cheaper cruiser Mk V, or A13 Mk III, subsequently dubbed Covenanter. This was the first of a long line of British tanks to be given names beginning with 'C' but the actual choice of this particular name is curious – apparently referring to a group of seventeenth-century Presbyterians who committed themselves to keeping their form of worship as the sole religion of Scotland, signing a covenant to this effect in 1638 and thus risking their lives.

Despite the Mk III designation, the Covenanter owed little to earlier versions of the A13 beyond the Christie suspension. The four-man vehicle had a redesigned hull with a lower profile, and incorporated increased thickness of armour. It had originally been planned that the hull would be welded, and the pilot model was constructed in this way, but a shortage of manpower and doubts about the strength of the welds led to a return to riveted construction using a sandwich of two plates. Nuffield Mechanizations also came up with a better-designed turret which used angular plates for improved performance against ballistics. The maximum thickness of armour was 40mm, giving a combat weight of 18 tons – this was more or less at the limit of the suspension, and led to unacceptable ground pressure.

The Nuffield Liberty engine of the earlier A13 variants was ousted in favour of a specially designed Meadows DAV tank engine, a horizontally-opposed twelve-cylinder unit producing 280–340bhp, that drove the rear sprockets. Also from Meadows, the transmission consisted of a four-speed gearbox together with a Wilson epicyclic steering unit; earlier plans to use a Wilson gearbox were abandoned due to fears about production. The width of the engine left little space in the engine compartment, and the radiators were positioned at the front, leading to cooling problems throughout the life of the vehicle. Top speed on the road was 30mph, reducing to 25mph when operated across country.

The 2-pounder (40mm) gun was retained, and secondary armaments included either one or a pair of 7.92mm Besa air-cooled machine guns.

A wooden mock-up was approved in late 1939 and production contracts were placed almost immediately, even before the first of two pilot models had been completed. The first of a total of 1,771 production vehicles appeared in late 1940. Production was undertaken by the LMS workshops, along with English Electric and Leyland under LMS design parentage. Although the Covenanter was used to re-equip the British 1st Armoured Division, the type never saw service outside the British Isles and was almost certainly never used in combat – although one example was destroyed by enemy action during an air raid!

The basic gun tank was produced in four variants in an attempt to solve the cooling problems: the Covenanter I was the original production version, and this was followed by the Covenanter II (cruiser tank Mk V*), III (cruiser tank Mk V**) and IV. A close-support version was produced with a 3in howitzer in place of the 2-pounder (40mm) gun, and a number of Covenanter I and II gun tanks were fitted with a 30-foot long hydraulically launched scissor bridge and used for training and development work. A Covenanter was also used for initial trials of the anti-mine roller attachment (AMRA), and a small number of obsolete vehicles were converted to observation post, armoured recovery and command vehicle roles.

Cruiser Tank Mk VI (A15) – Crusader

Following the abandonment of the A14 and A16 projects, Nuffield Mechanizations and Aero was asked to concentrate on the design of the A15, which, despite still being fitted with the 2-pounder (40mm) gun, was described as a heavy cruiser. Design work took place during 1938/39, and approval to construct a prototype and 200 production vehicles was given in July 1939, with the pilot to be delivered in March 1940. In order to speed the model into production, the design was based on the A13 Mk III, with the hull lengthened to include an additional wheel station to improve its ditch-crossing performance, and with the Meadows engine replaced by the V12 Liberty engine which had been used in the cruiser Mks III and IV and which was already in production. The transmission consisted of a four-speed gearbox, with a Wilson epicyclic steering unit.

There were three versions of the Crusader gun tank. Crusader I was the original production model, with a 2-pounder (40mm) gun mounted in an angular turret. There was also a front machine-gun turret, which was often removed in service, designed to mount a 7.92mm Besa machine gun; a second Besa machine gun was fitted in the turret, coaxial with the main gun. On the Crusader II (cruiser tank Mk VI A), the machine-gun turret was never fitted, but there was additional frontal armour on the hull and turret; on the Crusader III, the 2-pounder (40mm) gun was replaced by a 6-pounder (57mm) weapon, and the hull and turret armour were improved. Close-support versions of both the Crusader I and Crusader II were also produced, with a 3in howitzer replacing the 2-pounder. Other variants included a Crusader-based command vehicle and several types of anti-aircraft tanks mounting Bofors and Oerlikon weapons. Surplus and redundant Crusaders were also converted to the gun tractor, 'dozer, 'dozer/crane and armoured recovery vehicle roles, as well as being used for experimental work. A number of surplus Crusaders were fitted with the Rolls-Royce Meteor engine during the development of the Cromwell.

The Crusader was a low and compact design, with a riveted hull, and measured 236in long and 104in wide, with an overall height of 88in. The maximum thickness of armour was 40mm, subsequently upgraded to 49mm, and then 51mm, on the Crusaders II and III respectively. The turret was welded, with additional armour plates bolted to the sides. The battle weight of the Crusaders I and II was 19 tons, with the Crusader III tipping the scales at 19.75 tons; the radius of action was around 100 miles, or 125 miles with additional external fuel tanks.

The Crusader remained in production until 1943, by which time nine companies had been contracted to build a total of 5,300 vehicles under Nuffield's design parentage.

Cruiser Tank Mk VII (A24) – Cavalier

By late 1940, the inadequacies of earlier cruiser tanks had highlighted the desperate need to improve both the armour and the main gun, and a specification was drawn up for a new heavy cruiser tank. The specification called for a maximum thickness of armour of 65mm on the front of the hull, and 75mm on the turret front, which provided approximately 50 per cent more armour than the Crusader. The puny 2-pounder (40mm) gun was to be replaced by a 6-pounder (57mm), which required a larger turret and turret ring. It was also suggested that a new, more powerful engine be fitted to improve the maximum speed.

Three companies competed for the work. Vauxhall Motors proposed developing what would have been a scaled-down version of the Churchill infantry tank, designated A23, whilst both the Birmingham Railway Carriage and Wagon Company and Nuffield Mechanizations and Aero came up with a variation of the Crusader. Since the Crusader was already in production, Nuffield was asked to construct six pilot versions of a model described as the A24 by the autumn of 1941, with subsequent production provisionally allocated to Nuffield and Ruston and Hornsby. Nuffield had little choice but to use an uprated version of the old V12 Liberty engine already seen in the Crusader, though it now produced 410bhp in the Mk IV form. The design also shared the gearbox, Wilson epicyclic final drive and improved Christie suspension arrangements with the Crusader.

Whilst Nuffield had been busy with the pilot models, Leyland Motors, who were also constructing the Crusader, came up with their own proposal for a heavy cruiser based on work originally carried out by the Birmingham Railway Carriage and Wagon Company. This was effectively an improved Crusader chassis powered by a down-rated Rolls-Royce V12 Merlin 27-litre engine, which would become known as the Meteor, driving through the Merritt-Brown gearbox already being used in the Churchill. It was an attractive combination but, at the time, there was no spare production capacity for the engine, and the decision was taken to standardise subsequent cruiser tank designs on the improved chassis of the Leyland proposal, and subsequently to adopt the 600bhp Meteor engine as soon as was practicable.

The production version of the A24 was thus a combination of the hull of the proposed A27 Cromwell married to the power train, transmission and suspension of the Crusader. This resulted in some confusion with the name. The A24 was originally named Cromwell I – similarly, the Centaur (see below) was named Cromwell II – but the decision was subsequently taken to use this name for the A27, which came later, and so it was renamed Cavalier.

Measuring 240in in length and with a width of 113in, the hull was similar to the Crusader, providing space for a five-man crew, but the levels of armour were generally improved, resulting in a combat weight of 26.5 tons. The 6-pounder (57mm) main gun was mounted in a new six-sided boxy turret and there were both coaxial and hull-mounted 7.92mm Besa machine guns. Early examples used the Mk III 6-pounder (57mm), whilst later production was fitted with the Mk V version, the latter identifiable by the barrel counterweight. Maximum speed was 24mph on the road, and 14mph across country.

A total of 500 vehicles were ordered, 'sight unseen', in June 1941, the first being delivered the following January. By this time, the Cavalier was being considered an interim design whilst the development of the Meteor-engined A27 Cromwell was completed.

Cruiser Tank Mk VIII (A27L) – Centaur

Designated A27L to indicate that it was fitted with the Nuffield Liberty engine, and originally named Cromwell II, the Centaur was developed in response to continued delays with the Rolls-Royce Meteor engine. It was designed by Leyland Motors under the design parentage of the Birmingham Railway Carriage and Wagon Company, with design parentage for the whole A27 series transferred to Leyland Motors in November 1941.

The hull resembled the one already used for the Cavalier, with modified Christie suspension, and consisted of bolted armour on a riveted frame; the maximum thickness of armour was 76mm, resulting in a combat weight of 28.4 tons. The Centaur was capable of a top speed of 27mph on roads, and 16mph across country and the vehicle could accommodate a crew of five. Unlike the Cavalier, which was fitted with a manual gearbox and Wilson epicyclic steering unit, the Centaur was fitted with a Merritt-Brown gearbox and steering unit, as was intended for the Cromwell. Trials showed that the engine lacked sufficient power and reliability, however, and Leyland developed an uprated Mk V version for later production examples.

In its original form, the Centaur was fitted with the 6-pounder (57mm) gun, with a coaxial 7.92mm Besa machine gun; a second Besa machine gun was often fitted in a gimbal mount at the front of the hull, and many examples carried a .303in Bren gun for anti-aircraft defence. For the later Centaur III, the 6-pounder (57mm) gun was replaced by a 75mm weapon, making it more or less equivalent to the Cromwell IV, and large numbers of Centaur Is were converted to this configuration.

Centaur II was an experimental version with wider tracks, but there was no series production, whilst Centaur IV was equipped with a 95mm howitzer for the close-support role. Some 950 vehicles were constructed, eighty of them for the close-support.

In 1943, once the development work for the Meteor engine had been completed, a number of Centaurs were retrofitted with the new engine – they became known as the Cromwell X or, later, as Cromwell III. Others were converted to various other roles, including: artillery observation post, with a dummy gun fitted to the turret; anti-aircraft tank, with either an Oerlikon or Polsten gun; and 'dozer, armoured recovery vehicle or armoured personnel carrier – in all cases, with the turret removed.

Cruiser Tank (A27M) – Cromwell

Designed by the Birmingham Railway Carriage and Wagon Company, the first pilot model for the A27M Cromwell, in mild steel, was delivered for testing in March 1942. Two more pilot machines were completed by the end of the year, followed by a further twenty for training purposes. Design parentage was passed to Leyland Motors in late 1941.

Much of the Cromwell's success stemmed from the selection of the Rolls-Royce Meteor power unit. A down-rated but nevertheless powerful and reliable version of the famous 27-litre V12 Merlin aircraft engine, the Meteor shared some 80 per cent of its components with the Merlin, which greatly simplified production. It had been developed under the direction of Roy Robotham of Rolls-Royce specifically for use in tanks and made its first appearance during 1941 when two Crusaders, which the Cromwell was intended to replace, were experimentally fitted with the engine.

On early versions of the five-man Cromwell, the boxy hull and turret were constructed around a riveted frame onto which the armour was bolted, the large bosses on the turret providing a distinctive feature of the design. Later versions were of welded construction. The hull was 250in long and had a width of 115in; on the Cromwells VII and VIII, wider tracks pushed the width up to 120in. Like all of the A24 and A27 tanks, the suspension was of the improved Christie type with angled swinging arms suspended on long helical springs, the suspension units being fitted between the twin skins of the hull sides, giving a measure of protection from damage. There were five road wheels on each side, four of which were provided with shock absorbers.

The Meteor engine produced 600bhp from its 27 litres, and was installed in conjunction with the Merritt-Brown Z5 combined transmission and steering unit driving the rear sprockets. The engine gave the 27.5-ton tank a top speed on improved surfaces of 40mph, although this was subsequently governed to 32mph to reduce wear and tear on the running gear. The maximum speed across country was 18mph.

The A27M Cromwell and A27L Centaur variants have much in common, with several 'marks' of the Cromwell actually being re-engined Centaurs, in which the Liberty engine was replaced by the Meteor. The first version, the Cromwell I, was armed with a 6-pounder (57mm) main gun, together with a pair of Besa 7.92mm machine guns, one of which was coaxial to the main gun. A planned Cromwell II would have had wider tracks and lacked the hull machine gun, but none was produced. Cromwell III was a re-engined Centaur I, whilst Cromwell IV was a re-engined Centaur III, armed with a 75mm main gun capable of firing both high-explosive and anti-tank rounds – the War Office having decided to adopt the 75mm weapon as the main gun for tanks in January 1943. The Cromwell IVw was also equipped with the 75mm gun and was a converted Centaur but, as indicated by the 'w' suffix, had a welded hull; the Cromwell Vw was identical but was not converted from a Centaur. These were the first British tanks to be built with an all-welded hull. The Cromwell VI was a close-support variant, armed with a 95mm howitzer. Cromwell VII was an up-armoured version of either the Cromwell IV or V, fitted with wider tracks, stronger suspension and an altered final drive. Cromwell VIIw was a Cromwell Vw which had been rebuilt with the same modifications as the Cromwell VII and, finally, Cromwell VIII was a Cromwell VI rebuilt to the same standard as the Cromwell VII.

With the turret removed, the Cromwell was also used as the basis for an armoured recovery vehicle; other variants included an armoured observation post, with a dummy gun fitted, and a command vehicle. A few were also equipped with the Canadian indestructible roller device (CIRD) for exploding mines.

A total of 4,016 vehicles were constructed, and Cromwells saw their first action in June 1944 with reconnaissance regiments of the Royal Armoured Corps. The type is considered to be one of the most successful of the cruiser tanks and quickly proved to be fast, reliable and well protected. A number of Cromwells remained in service with the British Army into the post-war period.

Cruiser Tank (A30) – Challenger

The British Army's current main battle tank is the Challenger 2 and, if those who predict the death of the main battle tank are right, it may well be the last. Despite the name, there have actually been two previous British Challenger tanks. Challenger I was the direct predecessor of Challenger 2, but the original Challenger actually dates back to 1942 and was effectively an up-gunned and lengthened Cromwell designed to be able to defeat the heavier armour of the German tanks.

Three pilot models were developed by the Birmingham Railway Carriage and Wagon Company by lengthening and widening the Cromwell chassis, giving a length of 320in and a width of 115in. Stothert & Pitt came up with a new cast turret to accommodate the 17-pounder (76.2mm) gun, and a coaxial .30in Browning machine gun. Mechanically, the Challenger was little changed from the Cromwell, using the Rolls-Royce Meteor engine and David Brown five-speed transmission, as well as the improved Christie suspension. There were six road wheels on either side, rather than five, but the wheels were of slightly smaller diameter.

The first of these pilot machines was delivered in August 1942, but it would be fair to say that the design was not successful. The larger hull and turret, together with the 17-pounder (76.2mm) gun, increased the weight to more than 33 tons, more than four tons heavier than the Cromwell. This proved to be too much for the suspension. At the same time, the increased width also reduced mobility. The turret was very slow to traverse and, with the standard crew of five men – now without the planned second loader – the hull was very cramped, leading to the omission of the hull machine gun. In an attempt to overcome the defects, electric traversing gear was fitted and the thickness of armour on the turret was reduced to 63mm on the front and 40mm on the sides (compared to 75mm and 60mm on the Cromwell) in order to get the weight down to 32.5 tons. The armour on the hull was unchanged, at a maximum of 101mm. The final production version had a top speed on the road of 32mph, with a cross-country maximum of around 15mph.

A total of 200, or perhaps 260, vehicles were ordered in February 1943, with the first delivered in March 1944. Although the 17-pounder (76.2mm) gun was capable of matching the performance of the German 75mm and 88mm weapons, the Challenger was never really satisfactory and production ceased in November 1943. A planned Challenger II, with a lower turret, was abandoned at the prototype stage, but the original Challenger chassis was also used to produce the Avenger self-propelled gun.

Cruiser Tank (A34) – Comet

In 1944, the British Army finally got a heavy cruiser tank that was well protected, fast and well armed. Leyland Motors had been commissioned to develop a new cruiser tank in September 1942 following the British Army's experiences in the tank battles of the Western Desert. It had been clearly demonstrated that the British cruisers were totally outclassed by the German Panzers, particularly lacking sufficient firepower to cause any real damage to the better-armoured German machines. Leyland's brief was to design a new heavy cruiser tank that would incorporate as many features of the A27 design as possible. To assist in this, the design parentage for the A27 series was transferred to Leyland Motors at the beginning of 1943, though considerable work was still required to remedy the inadequacies of the existing design.

Work on producing a mock-up of the A34 started in July 1943 using a modified and better-protected Cromwell hull. Production was scheduled for mid-1944 and the first prototype appeared in February of that year. Power came from the 600bhp Rolls-Royce Meteor, driving through a David Brown Z5 five-speed transmission and, with a top speed on the road of 32mph and a cross-country maximum of 16mph, the Comet was fast and reliable. It was also well protected, with a maximum thickness of 102mm of armour on the hull front, bringing the battle weight of the tank up to 35.2 tons. Both the hull and turret were of welded construction, and the hull was 301in long and 120in wide, with sufficient space to comfortably accommodate a crew of five.

A larger gun had been high on the list of desirable improvements to enable the Comet to engage the German tanks on an equal basis. The obvious candidate was the 17-pounder (76.2mm) weapon but, since there was no question of being able to widen the hull, the decision was taken to adopt the Vickers HV (high velocity) 75mm (actually 76.2mm) gun, a design which had been developed speculatively by Vickers-Armstrongs. More compact and lighter than the 17-pounder (76.2mm) from which it was derived, the gun had a shorter barrel and breech but could be reconfigured to fire similar ammunition to that used in the 17-pounder (76.2mm), using a smaller shell casing, but with almost the same armour-penetrating performance. The new gun was described as the OQF 77mm Mk II (the 'O' standing for Ordnance, as in Royal Ordnance) to avoid confusion with existing guns. Alongside the main gun, there was a coaxial 7.92mm Besa machine gun, with a second similar weapon in the hull.

Total production amounted to 1,186 units and, whilst it might have arrived too late to have much effect on the outcome of the Second World War, the Comet offered a sufficiently impressive performance to remain in service for a further fifteen years or so.

The first pilot model for the A9 cruiser Mk I appeared in 1936, and the first of two contracts was placed the following year. Although the A9 incorporated some of the technical advances which had been planned for the abandoned medium tank Mk III, there were initial difficulties with the brakes, the suspension, the mounting of the main gun and the auxiliary machine-gun turrets. *(Warehouse Collection)*

Thirty-one A10 cruiser tank Mk IIs went to France with the British Expeditionary Force (BEF) in 1940. It was not successful and the War Office criticised the machine for being slow and underpowered, with a poor cross-country performance. *(Warehouse Collection)*

During 1941 the A10 saw action in North Africa and in Greece, where some sixty well-worn vehicles were found to perform well against the German tanks, with most subsequently succumbing to a catalogue of mechanical failure. Surprisingly, the suspension was found to work well in the desert. *(Warehouse Collection)*

A total of 175 units of the A10 were constructed during 1938 and 1939, with the Mk II A replacing the original Mk II after just thirteen models had been built. *(Warehouse Collection)*

The cruiser tank Mk III was developed by Morris Commercial Cars and constructed by Nuffield Mechanizations and Aero. It made much of what had gone before redundant and it was the first British tank to incorporate the Christie suspension system. The photograph shows one of the two prototypes constructed during 1937 and 1938, designated A13E2 and A13E3 – the original Christie tank was designated A13E1. *(Warehouse Collection)*

The last examples of the cruiser Mk III were delivered in the summer of 1940 and the type saw service with the 1st Armoured Division in France in 1940, as well as with the 7th Armoured Division in Libya in 1941. *(Warehouse Collection)*

The cruiser tank Mk IV was a logical development of the earlier Mk III, and a number of the earlier machines were subsequently up-armoured to Mk IV standard. *(Warehouse Collection)*

The main gun of the Mk IV was the 2-pounder (40mm), and there was also a coaxial Vickers .303in water-cooled machine gun, which on the Mk IV A was replaced by a Besa 7.92mm machine gun. *(Warehouse Collection)*

The cruiser tank Mk IV saw service in France in 1940, with many being abandoned at Calais, and in the desert war of 1940-41, where the relatively high speed was an asset. *(Warehouse Collection)*

Following their involvement with the A13 Mk II, in June 1937, the British government asked the workshops of the London Midland and Scottish Railway to assist with the design of the new A14 cruiser tank, which was to be powered by a Thornycroft marine engine, and the similar A16 (*seen here*), which was to be fitted with the Nuffield Liberty engine. Both were eventually abandoned in favour of the cruiser tank Mk V (A13 Mk III). *(Warehouse Collection)*

Although the Covenanter was used to re-equip the British 1st Armoured Division, the type never saw service outside the British Isles and was almost certainly never used in combat – although one example was destroyed by enemy action during an air raid! (*Warehouse Collection*)

The Covenanter was the first of a long line of British tanks to be given names beginning with 'C' – the actual name apparently referring to a group of seventeenth-century Presbyterians who committed themselves to keeping their form of worship as the sole religion of Scotland, signing a covenant to this effect in 1638 and thus risking their lives. This example is being carried on an American White 920 18-ton tank carrier. *(Tank Museum)*

Lacking its 2-pounder (40mm) main gun, this Covenanter has been loaded onto the trailer of a Scammell Pioneer TRMU30/TRCU30 tank transporter. Although it remained in service throughout the war, the Pioneer tank transporter was rated at just 30 tons and was subsequently superseded by the 40-ton Diamond T Model 980/981. *(Warehouse Collection)*

The design work for the Crusader (A15, cruiser tank Mk VI) took place during 1938/39, and approval to construct a prototype and 200 production vehicles was given in July 1939. The pilot model was delivered in March 1940. The contract was revised in mid-1940 to 400 vehicles, and then again to 1,062. (*Warehouse Collection*)

There were three versions of the Crusader gun tank. The Crusader I was the original version, with a 2-pounder (40mm) gun mounted in an angular turret. Crusader II (cruiser tank Mk VIA) omitted the machine-gun turret and had additional frontal armour on the hull and turret. Crusader III (*seen here*) had improved hull and turret armour and was armed with a 6-pounder (57mm) weapon. (*Simon Thomson*)

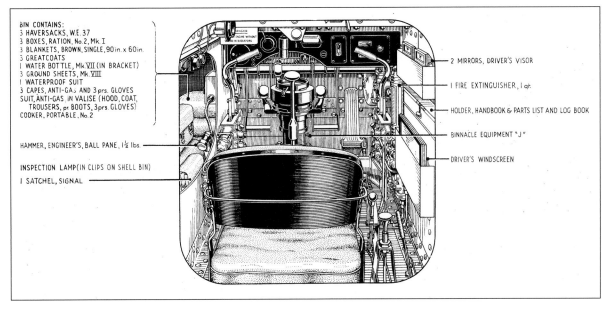

BIN CONTAINS:
3 HAVERSACKS, W.E. 37
3 BOXES, RATION, No. 2, Mk. I
3 BLANKETS, BROWN, SINGLE, 90 in. x 60 in.
3 GREATCOATS
1 WATER BOTTLE, Mk VII (IN BRACKET)
3 GROUND SHEETS, Mk. VIII
1 WATERPROOF SUIT
3 CAPES, ANTI-GAS AND 3 prs. GLOVES
SUIT, ANTI-GAS, IN VALISE (HOOD, COAT,
   TROUSERS, pr. BOOTS, 3 prs. GLOVES)
COOKER, PORTABLE, No. 2

HAMMER, ENGINEER'S, BALL PANE, 1½ lbs.

INSPECTION LAMP (IN CLIPS ON SHELL BIN)
1 SATCHEL, SIGNAL

2 MIRRORS, DRIVER'S VISOR

1 FIRE EXTINGUISHER, 1 qt.

HOLDER, HANDBOOK & PARTS LIST AND LOG BOOK

BINNACLE EQUIPMENT "J"

DRIVER'S WINDSCREEN

Stowage diagram for the driver's compartment of the Crusader I. *(Warehouse Collection)*

It was planned that the Crusader would be used to re-equip the British armoured divisions, and the type remained in production for four years, seeing its first action in the Western Desert in mid-1941. It was unable to match comparable German tanks in terms of armour and firepower and, although it was fast, with a maximum speed of 27mph, or better, on roads, and 15mph across country, it was never considered to be satisfactory and was frequently unreliable. The photograph shows the Crusader I with the original 2-pounder (40mm) gun. *(Warehouse Collection)*

Trials of the 6-pounder(57mm)-equipped Cavalier (A24, cruiser tank Mk VII) began in March 1942. The increased weight, due to a larger gun and thicker armour, meant that the tank was woefully underpowered, resulting in a short engine life and general problems with unreliability. It was almost immediately relegated to training duties and, although a few were used in northwest Europe as artillery observation posts, the type never saw active service as a gun tank. *(Warehouse Collection)*

Work on the design of the Centaur (A27L, cruiser tank Mk VIII) started in early 1941, and the first prototype was completed by June 1942. Here, Prime Minister Winston Churchill is shown the finer points of a Centaur III. *(Warehouse Collection)*

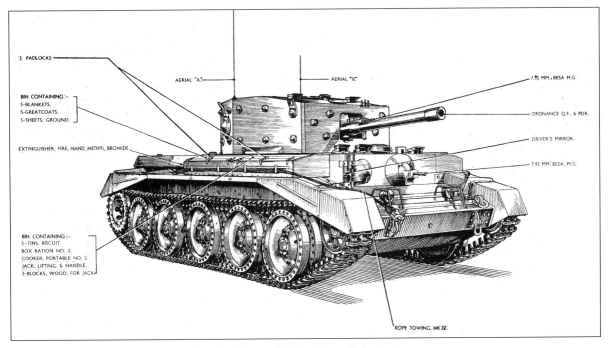

2 PADLOCKS

AERIAL "A."

AERIAL "B."

7.92 MM. BESA M.G.

BIN CONTAINING:—
5-BLANKETS.
5-GREATCOATS.
5-SHEETS, GROUND.

ORDNANCE Q.F., 6 PDR.

DRIVER'S MIRROR.

EXTINGUISHER, FIRE, HAND, METHYL, BROMIDE.

7.92 MM. BESA M.G.

BIN CONTAINING:—
5-TINS, BISCUIT.
BOX RATION NO. 3.
COOKER, PORTABLE NO. 2.
JACK, LIFTING, & HANDLE.
2-BLOCKS, WOOD, FOR JACK.

ROPE TOWING, MK IV.

External stowage diagram for the Centaur I. *(Warehouse Collection)*

Although based on the Cavalier, the radiators of the Centaur were repositioned and the engine compartment layout was modified to match more closely that of the Cromwell in order to simplify the replacement of the Liberty engine with a Meteor at a later date. *(Warehouse Collection)*

Most Centaurs were allocated to training, but eighty or so Centaur IVs were used by the Royal Marines armoured support regiments to provide cover for British and Commonwealth forces during the opening attacks of the D-Day landings. Firing onto the shore from landing craft before being driven inland, the tanks were operated by Royal Artillery crews, with the guns manned by Royal Marines – the turret sides were distinctively marked, following the principles of naval gunnery. This example is towing a Porpoise ammunition sledge. (Warehouse Collection)

Although it was actually designed by the Birmingham Railway Carriage and Wagon Company, the A27M Cromwell – it was also described as the Cromwell III and the Cromwell M – is more generally associated with Leyland Motors who had become the design parent for the A27 series in late 1941. The photograph shows the original Cromwell I. (Warehouse Collection)

The Cromwell IV was equipped with a 75mm main gun in place of the 6-pounder (40mm) original – although it was almost a match for the later German tanks, it doesn't seem to have helped this knocked-out unit much! *(Tank Museum)*

The Cromwell VI was a close-support variant, armed with a 95mm howitzer, and is the only version of the Centaur known to have seen any combat. Note how one of the crew members is leaning nonchalantly on the huge gun barrel counterweight. (Tank Museum)

The Cromwell VII was an up-armoured version of either the Cromwell IV or V, with wider tracks, stronger suspension and a final drive that reduced the maximum speed to 32mph. This example has become the victim of bitter street fighting in France. *(Tank Museum)*

Three pilot models for the A30 Challenger were developed by the Birmingham Railway Carriage and Wagon Company. Essentially a lengthened and widened version of the Cromwell, to which had been fitted a new cast turret to accommodate the 17-pounder (76.2mm) gun, it was designed to be able to defeat the heavier armour of the German tanks. *(Warehouse Collection)*

The turret of the Challenger was designed to accommodate two loaders, and included an unusual jacking feature that allowed any rounds which had jammed the unprotected turret base to be cleared. However, the turret was huge, giving the machine an overall height of 110in, compared to 98in for the Cromwell. The vehicle lacked the capacity to wade and was not used during the D-Day landings, but Challengers saw action with British reconnaissance regiments in north-west Europe in late 1944. *(Warehouse Collection)*

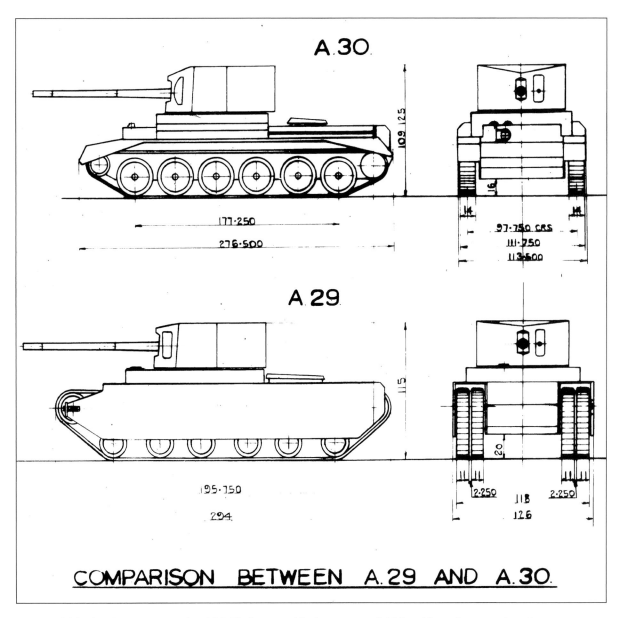

A.30.

A.29.

COMPARISON BETWEEN A.29 AND A.30.

This drawing compares the A30 Challenger with the proposed A29, a 45-ton heavy cruiser that was to have been armed with the 17-pounder (76.2mm) gun. The A29 did not progress beyond the drawing board and was abandoned in favour of the A30. *(Warehouse Collection)*

With its high-velocity 77mm gun, the A34 Comet was fast, well armed and well protected and finally gave the British Army a tank which could take on the better-protected and better-armed German tanks – but since it did not appear until six months after D-Day, and saw no real action until the Rhine crossings in March of the following year, it could be argued that it was almost too late! *(Simon Thomson)*

Although the track and suspension systems were ultimately redesigned and strengthened to include conventional return rollers, the Comet was based on the hull and running gear of the A27M Cromwell. There was a new, larger cast turret and a new turret ring, designed to accommodate a new Vickers 77mm gun and, even if it was not quite up to the performance of the 17-pounder(76.2mm)-equipped Sherman Firefly, the Comet was able to engage the German tanks on an equal basis. *(Warehouse Collection)*

Brand-new Comet pilot vehicle, in mild steel, photographed by its makers; note the lack of track-return rollers on the original Cromwell-style suspension. *(Warehouse Collection)*

Some examples of the Comet survived to see service in Korea in the early 1950s, and the last British Army Comet squadron was based in Hong Kong in 1960. Surplus Comets were sold to the armies of Finland, Burma and South Africa, as well as to the Irish Defence Force. *(Warehouse Collection)*

Chapter Four

Infantry Tanks

In 1934, General Sir Hugh Elles, Master-General of the Ordnance, asked Vickers-Armstrongs to design what was described as an 'infantry tank'. His brief asked that the vehicle be heavily protected, and armed with no more than a machine gun — and yet it was to be cheap and available in significant numbers. The weight of armour necessarily meant that the tank would be much slower than the so-called cruisers, but this was considered unimportant since the role of the infantry tank was to support slow-moving foot soldiers during an attack. Once the attack had broken through the enemy's front line, faster cruisers, or light tanks, would move in to consolidate the gains.

The design for the first of these infantry tanks, dubbed Matilda for its supposed resemblance to a cartoon duck, was the work of Sir John Carden. Despite being produced in two versions, it was not a great success, but Vickers was sufficiently encouraged by the Matilda to develop a design of their own as a private venture, reusing as many components as possible. The result was the Valentine, subsequently officially adopted as the infantry tank Mk III. It was said to be difficult to drive but, nevertheless, proved itself to be a reliable and robust design which was gradually improved and up-gunned over a four- or five-year period. Alongside the ubiquitous Valentine, the best known British infantry tank is almost certainly the Mk IV — better known as the Churchill. Designed by Harland and Wolff in 1940, and then redesigned for production by Vauxhall Motors, the Churchill remained in production until October 1945, with the last unit not being withdrawn from service until twenty years later.

Infantry Tank Mk I (A11) — Matilda I

The A11 was the first tank intended expressly for infantry support and was designed to a brief laid down by General Sir Hugh Elles for a small, well-armoured vehicle that would be relatively inconspicuous, and which could resist attack by the anti-tank guns of the period. The pilot model, designated A11E1, was submitted for trials in September 1936. It was an ungainly machine, consisting of a narrow, well-armoured riveted hull running on open tracks, with a length of 191in and a maximum thickness of 60mm, which made it invulnerable to any of the contemporary anti-tank guns. The driver was located centrally at the front and on top of the hull was mounted a tall, but cramped, one-man rotating turret of cast steel, armed with nothing more lethal than a Vickers .303in water-cooled machine gun – although this was later upgraded to a .50in gun, making the tiny turret even more cramped for the hapless gunner. The overall width was 90in, and the tank measured 74in to the top of the turret.

Power came from a 70bhp Ford V8 side-valve engine, driving the rear sprockets through a Ford four-speed gearbox; the brakes, clutches and steering system were adapted from those used on the Vickers light tanks. The suspension consisted of a pair of eight-wheeled leaf-sprung bogies on either side, with the return rollers positioned on the tops of the bogies. The top speed of the 11-ton machine across country was 5–6mph, which was, of course, faster than advancing infantry.

In 1937, Vickers was awarded a production contract for sixty machines, later increased to 139 (plus the prototype), and production continued until August 1940, by which time it was still one of the world's best-armoured tanks! Despite some Matildas going to France in 1940, the type saw little action, being used largely for training. By the end of 1936, work had started on designing its replacement, the A12 infantry tank Mk II.

Matilda I was also used to mount two types of early mine-clearance device – the Coulter mine plough and the Fowler rollers; neither device saw action.

Infantry Tank Mk II (A12) – Matilda II *et seq.*

It was obvious almost as soon as the Matilda I appeared that it was too small and was insufficiently armed. It was equally clear that the design could not be upgraded to mount a larger gun, nor to accommodate the minimum crew of three, without making the hull larger – and that this, in turn, would increase the weight and require a new more powerful engine. So, despite retaining the Matilda name – and being known either as Matilda Senior or Matilda II until the original Matilda was withdrawn – the infantry tank Mk II was a new design developed by the War Department Mechanization Board, a forerunner to the Department of Tank Design, and the Vulcan Foundry. The latter was responsible for producing the first wooden mock-up in November 1936, and the pilot machine, designated A12E1, in April 1938.

The hull was larger, with a maximum thickness of 78mm, and there were heavy side skirts to protect the tracks and the suspension. The turret was hydraulically operated and the gun was stabilised. Motive power was provided by a pair of AEC six-cylinder diesel engines, each producing 87bhp, linked together and driving through a six-speed Wilson epicyclic gearbox; steering was effected by a Rackham clutch and brake system. In the later Matilda III, the AEC engines were replaced by Leyland six-cylinder diesels, with a combined power output of 190bhp. The suspension was of the bell-crank 'Japanese' type using compound helical springs, the design of which was borrowed from the A6 six-tonner. The 221in-long hull provided accommodation for a four-man crew, and the maximum speed of the 26.5-ton machine on roads was 15mph, reducing to 11mph across country.

The main gun was the 2-pounder (40mm), but there was also a close-support variant mounting a 3in howitzer. A Vickers .303in water-cooled machine gun, and later a 7.92mm Besa machine gun, was carried in a coaxial mount. There were smoke dischargers on either side of the turret and most tanks also carried a .303in Bren gun for anti-aircraft defence.

Production contracts were placed straight off the drawing board in June 1938, with Vulcan Foundry producing most of the castings for the hull and turret, and undertaking final assembly. Fowlers, Ruston and Hornsby, Harland and Wolff, North British Locomotive and the London Midland Scottish Railway workshops were also involved and the total number produced was 2,987, in five main variants. Matilda I* (infantry tank Mk II) was the first production variant, with AEC engines and a 2-pounder (40mm) gun. For the Matilda II (infantry tank Mk IIA), the Vickers machine gun was replaced by a 7.92mm Besa weapon. With the Leyland engines in place of the AEC units the designation became Matilda III (infantry tank Mk IIA*) and when the original Leyland E148/148 engines were replaced by the E164/165 units, the designation was changed to Matilda IV (infantry tank Mk IIA**). Finally, Matilda V (infantry tank Mk II) incorporated improvements to the gearbox and the gear-change mechanism.

There was also a close-support version of the Matilda III and IV, with a 3in howitzer in place of the 2-pounder (40mm). Matildas were also adapted for a variety of specialised roles including mine clearance (Baron, Fowler roller and Scorpion), bridgelayer (Inglis), trench-crossing device and canal defence light (Matilda II and Matilda V CDL). The Australian Army also fitted Matildas with the Frog and Murray flame-thrower devices, as well as a box 'dozer blade.

The Matilda's general lack of speed and rather clumsy steering system, together with an inability to fire high-explosive ammunition, meant that the type was rendered obsolete by the appearance of the Valentine (infantry tank Mk III), and by the US-built M3 Grant and M4 Sherman. However, this was not the end of the Matilda's service career and a number served with the Australian Army in the Far East where the armour was suitably effective against Japanese guns.

Infantry Tank Mk III, III* – Valentine

Valentine was a private venture by Vickers-Armstrongs, designed largely by Leslie Little as an alternative to the A10, but, having been shown drawings of the machine, the War Office was said to have been unhappy about the size of the turret and it was more than a year before a contract was issued. However, when the first order for 275 vehicles was placed in July 1940, the demand for tanks to replace those abandoned following the evacuation of the British Expeditionary Force from France and Belgium was so pressing that the need for a pilot model was waived. Construction started in July 1939, with the first of what ended up as a total of 8,275 vehicles being delivered in May 1940 ready for trials. Despite being designed as an infantry tank, with a maximum thickness of armour of just 65mm, a shortage of cruisers meant that the Valentine soon found itself equipping the newly raised armoured divisions as well as supporting tank brigade infantry.

Valentine I was equipped with an AEC A179 six-cylinder petrol engine producing around 135bhp from 9,610cc, although this was subsequently replaced by the uprated A189 version. In Valentines II and III (infantry tank Mk III*), the petrol engine was replaced by an AEC A190 Comet Mk III six-cylinder diesel engine with a power output of 145bhp from the same 9,610cc capacity – although often dismissed as a 'bus engine', the A190 was actually developed specifically for the Valentine. All subsequent versions used an American GMC 6004 two-stroke diesel engine with a power output of 210bhp. In all cases, the engine was coupled to a five-speed transmission driving the rear sprockets. There were six road wheels on either side, carried in two bogies, with the leading and trailing wheels of larger diameter than the others; suspension was of the 'slow motion' pattern. The hull was riveted and was designed to accommodate a three-man crew (later four), measuring 212in in length and 103in wide, with the length extended to 232in from Valentine VIII. The combat weight was 17.4 tons, rising to 18.3 tons from Valentine VIII, and the intended infantry support role meant that the top speed was pegged at just 15mph on road surfaces, and 8mph across country.

Valentines I to VII were armed with the 2-pounder (40mm), generally with a co-axial 7.92mm Besa machine gun; for Valentines VIII to X, the main gun was replaced by the 6-pounder (57mm), and from Valentine VI, the Besa machine gun was replaced by a Browning .30in gun. The final derivative, the Mk XI, carried a 75mm gun.

A number served as command vehicles with anti-tank brigades, but by the time the larger and more heavily armoured Churchill infantry tank started to be available in quantity, the Valentine was beginning to show its age. However, production of Valentines continued until 1944 and, with plenty of serviceable vehicles available, the

Valentine hull was often chosen as the basis for various specialised roles. These included canal defence light (CDL), duplex-drive (DD) amphibious assault tank, Scorpion mine-clearance flail, anti-mine roller attachment, Snake mine exploder, observation/command post, flame-thrower, flame mortar, bridgelayer or armoured ramp carrier (Ark). The Valentine hull was also used as the basis of the Archer 17-pounder (76.2mm) and Bishop 25-pounder (87.6mm) self-propelled guns.

Although it was cramped and hard to drive, the Valentine was reliable and robust and was well liked by its crews. The tank saw its first service during Operation Crusader in North Africa, and was widely used in the Western Desert in 1941, in Tunisia and Madagascar, as well as with the New Zealand Army in the Pacific.

By the time Valentine production ended, 6,855 vehicles had been manufactured in Britain, by Vickers-Armstrongs, Metropolitan-Cammell Railway Carriage and Wagon Company, and the Birmingham Railway Carriage and Wagon Company; a further 1,420 were constructed in Canada by the workshops of the Canadian Pacific Railway (Valentines VI, VII and VIIA). Most of the latter went to the Soviet Union, where they were used during the Battle of Moscow.

Infantry Tank Mk IV (A22) – Churchill

With a total of 5,640 units – some sources suggest even more – constructed over a five-year period, the Churchill was the second most numerous British tank of the Second World War. Once the initial teething problems had been solved it also became one of the most reliable. Unfortunately, although it was well armoured, as with most Allied tanks its firepower was sadly inadequate when confronted with the German 75mm and 88mm guns.

The work that eventually led to the development of the A22 Churchill started in September 1939 when the Belfast shipyard of Harland and Wolff was commissioned to construct four prototypes for a new infantry tank designated A20. The prototypes were completed by June 1940 and were powered by a twelve-cylinder Meadows engine, which quickly proved itself to be insufficiently powerful. The vehicle was also plagued by transmission troubles.

By this time, events in France had shown that this would be a war of movement and that notions of trench warfare should be forgotten. Clearly, the A20 was obsolete but, using the best features of the design as a starting point, H. E. Merritt, the Director of Tank Design, drew up a specification for yet another infantry tank, this time designated A22. Now there was a new twist to the equation – the shortages of equipment resulting from the abandonment of so much materiel on the beaches of northern France and Belgium dictated a tight timescale and the War Office insisted that the A22 be ready for production within twelve months. Vauxhall

Motors had been working on a horizontally opposed twelve-cylinder engine to replace the Meadows unit of the A20, and it was decided to move the A22 development work from Harland and Wolff to Vauxhall. To save time, Vauxhall retained the basic Harland and Wolff hull and the sprung-bogie suspension. The Bedford flat-twelve engine was also retained, producing 325–350bhp from a capacity of 21,240cc and driving the rear sprockets via a Merritt-Brown five-speed gearbox and epicyclic steering unit – although after just 100 vehicles had been constructed, the five-speed transmission was replaced by a four-speed unit. The first pilot model was ready by November 1940.

The hull was of composite construction, consisting of an outer covering of armour plate bolted to a mild-steel inner skin, giving a maximum thickness of armour of 102mm; on the later Mks VII and VIII versions, the thickness of armour was increased to 152mm. The first version was fitted with a cast turret, but this was later superseded by a larger turret of either cast, welded or composite construction.

It was a large and relatively heavy machine – the hull measured 293in in length and was 100in wide, with the width increased to 108in from the Mk III onwards, but at least there was plenty of room for the five-man crew. The combat weight was 39 tons, rising to 40 tons for the Mks VII and VIII and this held the top speed down to around 17mph, reducing to 12.5mph for the heavier Mks VII and VIII.

The first two variants were armed with the 2-pounder (40mm) gun in a cast turret, with a coaxial 7.92mm Besa machine gun and a 3in howitzer mounted in the nose, although in the Churchill II the howitzer was replaced by a second Besa machine gun. There was also a Churchill II close-support version with the 3in howitzer in the turret and the 2-pounder in the nose. When the Churchill III appeared in March 1942, it was sporting the harder-hitting 6-pounder (57mm) in a new welded turret; on the Churchill IV the turret was cast. A Churchill IV(NA) version was constructed in North Africa, with the 6-pounder (57mm) replaced by an M3 75mm gun salvaged from battle-damaged Shermans. Churchill VI was a converted IV, fitted with a 75mm gun developed by Vickers-Armstrongs; tanks manufactured with this gun were designated Churchill VII, or A22F. Churchill V and VIII were close-support versions, with the 6-pounder (57mm) gun replaced by a 95mm howitzer.

Other variants included the Churchill IX, which was a reworked III or IV with a new turret and 6-pounder (57mm) gun, and the Churchill IX-LT, armed with the same gun but retaining the original turret. Churchills X and X-LT were reworked in the same way as the IX, but were armed with the 75mm gun, and Churchills XI and XI-LT were Churchill Vs with additional appliqué armour and the 75mm gun.

The Churchill Oke was developed for use as a flame-thrower in 1942, based on the Churchill II. Further trials with Valentine flame-throwers led to the Churchill

Crocodile, initially based on the Churchill IV but, when it came to production, using the Churchill VII instead. Fuel for the flame-thrower was carried in a pressurised trailer and was passed to the hull through an articulated coupling; the projector for the petroleum-based fuel replaced the hull machine gun and the trailer could be remotely detached once the fuel was consumed, allowing reversion to the original role of a gun tank. Other Churchill adaptations included: armoured recovery vehicle (ARV) and deep-wading beach armoured recovery vehicle (BARV); three types of Ark (armoured ramp carrier); hydraulic bridgelayer; bobbin mat layers; various types of mechanical and explosive mine-clearance devices; and the Ardeer Aggie and Woodpecker *Pétard* mortar projectors.

Production was carried out by a consortium of manufacturers led by Vauxhall Motors. Alongside Vauxhall, other participants included Broom and Wade, Birmingham Railway Carriage and Wagon Company, Metropolitan-Cammell, Leyland Motors, Dennis Brothers, Harland and Wolff, Gloucester Railway Carriage and Wagon Company, Newton, Chambers and Company, and Beyer Peacock and Company. The last Churchill was built in October 1945.

The Churchill's first action was with the Canadian Army in the Dieppe raid of August 1942, although there was little opportunity to see how it performed. It was also used in Italy, North Africa and northwest Europe, and after the war was used in Korea where it saw its last service as a gun tank. Some specialised versions remained in service until 1965. Churchills were also supplied to the armies of Australia and the Soviet Union during the Second World War, and surplus Churchills were sold or gifted to Ireland, India and Jordan.

Infantry Assault Tank (A38) – Valiant
Intended for use in the Far East as an infantry assault tank, the A38 Valiant used as many Valentine components as possible but carried a new, larger turret, mounting either a 6-pounder (57mm) or 75mm gun, together with a single coaxial 7.92mm Besa machine gun. Although similar in general layout, at 211in long and 111in wide, the four-man hull was larger than the Valentine, and was constructed from heavier cast sections, with a maximum thickness of 110mm, and with a new cast nose that offered considerably greater protection. The turret was also larger and wider, and was bolted together from large cast plates.

The first prototype appeared in 1944, but proved to be extremely difficult to drive during trials. By this time the design was considered obsolete anyway and there was no series production. A second prototype – Valiant II – was planned, and possibly produced, using a Rolls-Royce V8 Meteorite petrol engine (effectively a shortened version of the V12 Meteor) in place of the GMC diesel, but again nothing came of the project.

Like later marks of Valentine, power was provided by a GMC 6004 six-cylinder two-stroke diesel engine, producing 210bhp and driving through an AEC gearbox. Unlike those on the Valentine, the road wheels were all of the same diameter and were individually suspended. With a combat weight of 27 tons, some 10 tons greater than the Valentine, the speed was restricted to just 12mph.

Infantry Tank (A43) – Black Prince

In 1943, Vauxhall Motors was asked to develop an improved version of the Churchill infantry tank capable of mounting a 17-pounder (76.2mm) gun. The hull of the Churchill VII/VIII was the starting point, with the length increased to 347in and the width to 136in, which, despite the larger gun, must have provided a little more space for the crew of five. The running gear consisted of the Bedford flat-twelve petrol engine of the Churchill, combined with a Merritt-Brown H52 five-speed transmission and a differential steering system. Although the maximum thickness of armour was unchanged at 152mm, the changes to the length of the vehicle, combined with the use of a larger gun, put the weight up to 50 tons and reduced the maximum speed on roads to 11mph, with 7mph across country. There was an all-new cast turret, mounting the 17-pounder (76.2mm) main gun, together with a pair of 7.92mm Besa machine guns, one mounted coaxially in the turret. Just six prototypes were constructed – and none saw any action.

The budget allocated to Vickers for production of the A11 infantry tank Mk I called for a maximum price of £6,000, which restricted the designers to producing a two-man tank. It was designed by Sir John Carden at Vickers-Armstrongs in 1934/35. *(Warehouse Collection)*

Early trials showed that the Matilda had a tendency to throw tracks and this was resolved on production machines by relocating the track-return rollers on the sides of the hull. Changes were also made to the layout of the nose. A small number of Matildas went to France in 1940, but were mostly confined to training. *(Warehouse Collection)*

Looking nothing like its predecessor, the Matilda II was based largely on the A7 medium tank that had been designed at the Royal Ordnance Factory (Woolwich) in 1929, but which had never gone into production. *(Warehouse Collection)*

Matildas II–V saw action with the 7th Royal Tank Regiment as part of the British Expeditionary Force (BEF) in France in 1940, where the thickness of the hull led the Germans to reconsider the calibre of their anti-tank guns, and in the Western Desert, where it proved equally resistant to Italian anti-tank weapons. The photograph shows a Matilda IIA belonging to the Tank Museum. *(Simon Thomson)*

Although it used mechanical components borrowed from the Vickers-built cruiser tanks Mks I and II, it is something of a sad indictment of official War Office tank design that the most numerous British tank of the Second World War – the Valentine – was actually a private venture by Vickers-Armstrongs. It is said to have acquired its name by virtue of having been presented to the War Office on 12 February 1938 – two days short of St Valentine's Day – though the name may also have been derived from Vickers-Armstrongs Limited, Elswick, Newcastle-upon-Tyne. *(Warehouse Collection)*

This photograph shows a Valentine II fitted with sand shields and auxiliary fuel tanks for long-range desert use in the Middle East. Valentine III had a larger turret with space for a third crew member and Valentines VI, VII and VIIA were constructed in Canada, using a cast rather than riveted nose. *(Warehouse Collection)*

External stowage diagram for the Valentine IX. *(Warehouse Collection)*

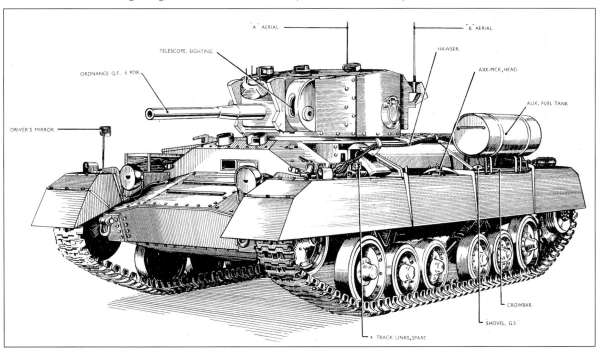

The Valentine was selected as the development platform for the duplex-drive (DD) amphibious assault tank. The wading screen is collapsed down onto the hull in this photograph. *(Simon Thomson)*

The Valentine IX was effectively a Valentine V up-gunned with the 6-pounder (57mm); at the same time, the turret crew was reduced to two. *(Warehouse Collection)*

Although it was cramped and hard to drive, the Valentine was reliable and robust and was well liked by its crews. The tank saw its first service during Operation Crusader in North Africa, and was widely used in the Western Desert in 1941, and in Tunisia and Madagascar, as well as with the New Zealand Army in the Pacific. The photograph shows a Valentine IX. *(Simon Thomson)*

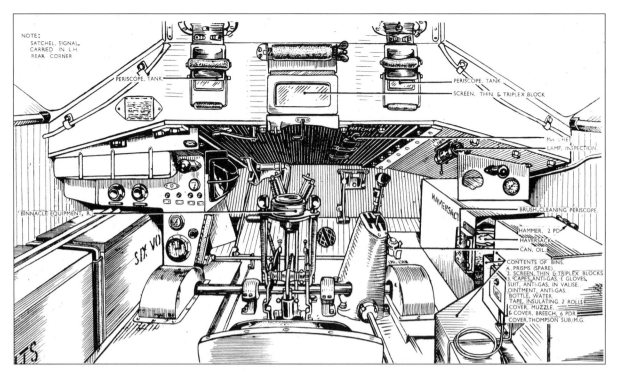

Stowage diagram for the Valentine driving compartment. *(Warehouse Collection)*

In all, 650 Valentine III and VIII tanks were converted for duplex-drive (DD) operation and were used for crew training. *(Simon Thomson)*

The A22 Churchill infantry tank was derived from this Harland and Wolff prototype for what was described as the A20. With its rhomboidal hull harking back to the designs of the First World War, the A20 was intended to have good trench-crossing abilities, and was to be armed with a pair of 2-pounder (40mm) guns, one mounted in the turret, the other in the nose; machine guns were planned for recesses in the hull sides. It was obsolete before it was completed. *(Warehouse Collection)*

Vauxhall's A22 Churchill superseded the A20 and the War Office approved the design immediately, believing that any problems – and there were many – could be ironed out whilst production was under way. A contract was issued for 500 tanks and the first fourteen production vehicles, designated Churchill I, were delivered by June 1941. *(Tank Museum)*

The Churchill's exposed tracks were wrapped around the perimeter of the hull and were supported on eleven small steel road wheels, each with its own trailing arm and coil-spring suspension; track covers were fitted from May 1942, with early vehicles reworked. *(Warehouse Collection)*

The Churchill underwent considerable development during its production life, with eight major variants and its heavy armour, roomy hull and regular shape also made it useful as an engineer's vehicle, with innumerable adaptations and modifications for specialised roles. The nose-mounted 3in howitzer was featured only on the Churchill I. *(Warehouse Collection)*

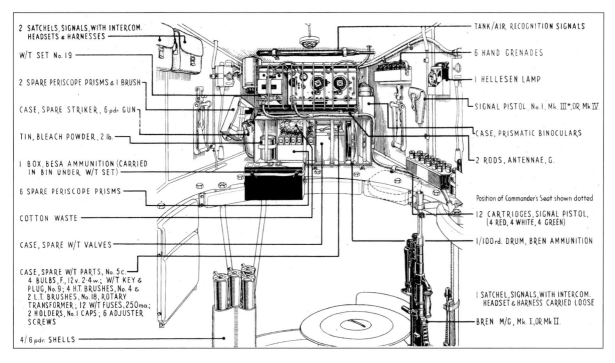

2 SATCHELS, SIGNALS, WITH INTERCOM.
HEADSETS & HARNESSES

W/T SET No. 19

2 SPARE PERISCOPE PRISMS & 1 BRUSH

CASE, SPARE STRIKER, 6 pdr. GUN

TIN, BLEACH POWDER, 2 lb.

1 BOX, BESA AMMUNITION (CARRIED
IN BIN UNDER W/T SET)

6 SPARE PERISCOPE PRISMS

COTTON WASTE

CASE, SPARE W/T VALVES

CASE, SPARE W/T PARTS, No. 5c.
4 BULBS, F., 12 v. 2·4 w.; W/T KEY &
PLUG, No. 9; 4 H.T. BRUSHES, No. 4 &
2 L.T. BRUSHES, No. 18, ROTARY
TRANSFORMER; 12 W/T FUSES, 250 ma.;
2 HOLDERS, No. 1 CAPS; 6 ADJUSTER
SCREWS

4/6 pdr. SHELLS

TANK/AIR RECOGNITION SIGNALS

6 HAND GRENADES

1 HELLESEN LAMP

SIGNAL PISTOL, No. 1, Mk. III*, OR Mk. IV.

CASE, PRISMATIC BINOCULARS

2 RODS, ANTENNAE, G.

Position of Commander's Seat shown dotted

12 CARTRIDGES, SIGNAL PISTOL,
(4 RED, 4 WHITE, 4 GREEN)

1/100 rd. DRUM, BREN AMMUNITION

1 SATCHEL, SIGNALS, WITH INTERCOM.
HEADSET & HARNESS CARRIED LOOSE

BREN M/G, Mk. I, OR Mk. II.

Stowage diagram for the Churchill III turret. *(Warehouse Collection)*

The Churchill IV was armed with a 6-pounder (57mm) gun in a new design of cast turret. *(Warehouse Collection)*

Intended for the close-support role, the Churchill V was equipped with a 95mm howitzer in place of the 6-pounder (57mm) gun. *(Warehouse Collection)*

Churchills which were fitted with the Vickers 75mm gun during construction were designated Churchill VII, or A22F, and also featured increased thickness of armour and a new cast and welded turret. Tanks which were retro-fitted with this gun in place of the 6-pounder (57mm) were designated Churchill VI. *(Warehouse Collection)*

Lacking its 6-pounder gun, this Churchill IV is being put through a submersion test – making the driver look extremely nervous. (Warehouse Collection)

Early Churchill III, battle-damaged and being inspected by *Wehrmacht* troops. Note how the left-hand track is completely missing. *(Warehouse Collection)*

Churchill VII (A22F) photographed during production at Luton; the turret is about to be united with the hull. *(Warehouse Collection)*

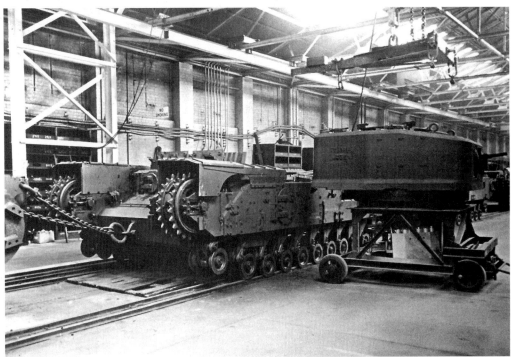

The proposed A28 infantry tank would have been constructed from parts of the A27M Cromwell. The project was initiated by Rolls-Royce, but was abandoned in December 1941. *(Warehouse Collection)*

Initiated in 1943 by Vickers-Armstrongs as a way of producing a more capable version of the Valentine, the design work for the A38 Valiant was carried out by the Birmingham Railway Carriage and Wagon Company, and the prototypes were constructed by Ruston and Hornsby. *(Warehouse Collection)*

The Black Prince was effectively an upgraded Churchill armed with the 17-pounder (76.2mm) gun. It was only ever considered to be an interim project whilst development of the A41 Centurion was completed and the contract was cancelled in May 1945 when the war in Europe ended. *(Warehouse Collection)*

Seen here with the turret traversed to the rear, the A43 Black Prince shows the modified Churchill coil-spring suspension which was improved to support the increased weight. *(Warehouse Collection)*

With the hull widened and lengthened, putting the weight up to some 50 tons, the Black Prince – sometimes dubbed the 'Super Churchill' – rode on wider 24in tracks. *(Warehouse Collection)*

Chapter Five

Heavy Tanks

During the later years of the interwar period most tank experts felt that the day of the heavy tank was over. Since 1938, British tank strategy had called for a mix of well-armed and well-protected infantry tanks to assist in breaking through enemy lines, together with fast, lightly gunned and lightly armoured cruiser tanks which could exploit breaks in the line and rampage at will, causing havoc in the enemy's rear areas.

However, when Britain declared war on Germany in 1939 there were those who foresaw a return to the trench warfare of the earlier conflict. If this were the case, then heavy tanks would be required once again, with the emphasis on their trench-crossing performance. The speed with which the German *Wehrmacht* conducted their *Blitzkrieg* campaigns across Belgium and France, with highly mobile tanks and infantry working together to keep the enemy off-balance, soon put paid to this notion – but not before Britain had designed a pair of heavy tanks.

The heavy tank did not become an issue again until the latter years of the conflict and by this time, it was the twin imperatives of firepower and protection that were driving the development.

Heavy Tank – TOG

During the early years of the Second World War, Sir Albert Stern, who had played a part in designing tanks during the previous conflict, gathered together some former associates and set about designing a tank capable of operating across the typical shelled and waterlogged ground that had formed the front line in 1914. Design work started in February 1940, and William Foster & Company of Lincoln was selected for production.

Dubbed TOG – for 'the old gang' – the first prototype, TOG I, was ready for trials in October 1940. It was powered by a 600bhp Paxman-Ricardo twelve-cylinder diesel engine driving electric motors via a pair of generators, and was capable of a maximum speed of 8.5mph, although the length of track made steering something of a challenge. The original design had included sponson-mounted guns, but by the time the first prototype had been constructed these had been superseded and were replaced by the turret of a Matilda II mounting a 2-pounder (40mm), together with a bow-mounted 17-pounder (76.2mm).

TOG I was subsequently fitted with a Fluidrive hydraulic drive system, when it was redesignated TOG IA; a second prototype, TOG II, appeared in March 1941, using the diesel-electric drive system of TOG I, but with torsion-bar suspension and lower tracks. Initially, TOG II was fitted with a dummy 77mm gun and turret, but this was replaced by a Stothert & Pitt turret with Metadyne traversing gear, carrying a 6-pounder (57mm). In the subsequent TOG II* this was replaced by a 17-pounder (76.2mm). A planned TOG IIR variant, which would have been shorter, was never completed.

Needless to say, there was no series production.

Heavy Assault Tank (A33)

The A33 heavy assault tank was an attempt to produce a standard or 'universal' tank chassis designed for a crew of five, which could be adapted to both the infantry and cruiser roles. Two prototypes were constructed by English Electric in 1943, against competition from Rolls-Royce, before the project was abandoned.

The basis of the tank was an up-armoured A27 hull, with a maximum thickness of 114mm, giving a considerable combat weight of 45 tons. The engine was the 27-litre V12 Rolls-Royce Meteor, producing 600bhp, driving the rear sprockets through a five-speed Merritt-Brown transmission with steering through a controlled differential. Although both prototypes were armed with the ubiquitous 6-pounder (57mm) gun, with both coaxial and hull-mounted 7.92mm Besa machine guns, it was envisaged that, if the tank eventually went into production, the main gun would be replaced by the 75mm weapon.

The work was terminated in May 1944.

Heavy Assault Tank (A39) – Tortoise

In 1942, the War Office initiated the development of a heavy tank destroyer that would be able to penetrate easily the armour of all other tanks and tank destroyers of the period, without putting itself at risk. In order to avoid what was described as the 'vicious circle of power and speed demanding heavier suspensions, leading to more weight, more track area, greater length, and more power', the Department of Tank Design (DTD) decided that it would abandon all conventional tank design considerations and approach the basic layout with a completely open mind.

Design work was initiated by Nuffield Mechanizations and Aero in 1944, with a view to having the first vehicle ready by 1945. General arrangement drawings and a detailed specification were prepared in 1944, followed by a full-size wooden mock-up for approval, and, by 1947 Nuffield had built six running prototypes. By any standards, the Tortoise was a huge, lumbering beast. The one-piece cast hull provided accommodation for a crew of seven, and measured up at 285in in length, with an overall width, including the track guards, of 147in. The lack of a conventional turret saved a considerable amount of weight, but also allowed the designers to build more strength and integrity into the hull since there was no need for a turret ring – always a weak area. Nevertheless, it was 230mm thick at its maximum, and the vehicle weighed 78 tons.

Power came from a Rolls-Royce Meteor 600bhp 27-litre V12 petrol engine driving the front sprockets through a Merritt-Brown six-speed gearbox. The drive sprockets were protected by huge armoured castings, and the track guards were made of 25mm-thick armoured steel. There was torsion-bar suspension, with eight wheel stations per side.

The main gun, a 32-pounder (94mm) weapon derived from a naval anti-aircraft gun, was carried in a huge 24in-diameter ball mount and, with a muzzle velocity of 3,050ft/sec, this was the most powerful gun to be fitted to a British tank up to that time. Secondary armaments included a 7.92mm Besa machine gun carried in a ball mounting on the left-hand side of the glacis plate, with a pair of similar weapons in a roof cupola for anti-aircraft defence.

Whilst the Tortoise embraced the principles of firepower and protection whole-heartedly it was almost certainly at the expense of mobility – top speed on the road was quoted as 12mph, with 4mph achievable across country, and the range was just twenty-eight miles on the road. The sheer size and lack of manoeuvrability of the machine ensured that it would have been of very limited tactical value, and the project was abandoned soon after the delivery of the prototypes.

With tracks running around its perimeter, the 400in-long hull of what was dubbed 'TOG' had some similarities with the familiar rhomboid tanks of the First World War, and was constructed from twin cement-bonded steel plates with a maximum thickness of 76mm. The tank was initially fitted with the turret of a Matilda II mounting a 2-pounder (40mm) gun, together with a bow-mounted 17-pounder (76.2mm) which was later to be fitted to the Challenger. In TOG II* form, as seen here, the 17-pounder gun was fitted into a conventional turret. *(Tank Museum)*

Just two examples of TOG were constructed and, whilst it would be fair to wonder 'what were they thinking?', the series was apparently only abandoned because the 80-ton combat weight was considered to be excessive. The photograph shows the TOG II*, which has survived at the Tank Museum. *(Warehouse Collection)*

Described as a heavy assault tank, the A33 was intended to provide a 'universal' tank chassis that could be adapted to both the infantry and cruiser roles. It was constructed on an up-armoured A27 hull, and was powered by the 27-litre V12 Rolls-Royce Meteor engine. *(Warehouse Collection)*

The first of the A33 prototypes (*seen here*) used the track and horizontal volute spring suspension (HVSS) of the American M6 heavy tank, whilst the second (designated A33-R/L) used a widened version of the A27 Cromwell tracks, with suspension designed by the LMS workshops. The rear view shows the auxiliary fuel tanks and air intakes for the Rolls-Royce engine. *(Warehouse Collection)*

With its 32-pounder (94mm) main gun and 225mm-thick cast hull, the A39 Tortoise heavy assault tank was designed to take on the fearsome German tank hunters – the *SdKfz.173 Jagdpanther*, which was armed with the 88mm *PaK L/71* gun; the *SdKfz.181* Tiger tank with its 88mm *KwK36 L/56* gun; and the 128mm *PaK44*-equipped *SdKfz.186 Jagdtiger. (Warehouse Collection)*

There were massive problems in transporting the A39 Tortoise on the road, with trials in Germany indicating that a minimum of two Diamond T tractors were required. *(IWM, MVE 136162)*

Here, Tortoise prototype number 1 has been loaded onto one of Pickfords' 100-ton girder trailers, supplied by Cranes, supported on a pair of two-line solid-tyred bogies. The two Scammell drawbar tractors that are visible would have been sufficiently powerful to move the 78-ton Tortoise plus the dead weight of the trailer, but probably only on metalled surfaces. *(IWM, MVE 9902-3)*

Chapter Six

American Tanks in British Service

In May 1940, following the successful evacuation of the British Expeditionary Force (BEF) from the beaches of northern France and Belgium, huge quantities of equipment, including tanks, wheeled vehicles and self-propelled guns, were abandoned. Although much was deliberately destroyed, some of this equipment fell into German hands.

The evacuation, Operation Dynamo, started on 27 May and by 4 June 338,226 British and French soldiers had been rescued by a fleet of 850 boats. When the operation ended the army was forced to leave 2,472 guns, almost 65,000 vehicles – including more than 400 tanks and 20,000 motorcycles – 416,000 tons of stores, more than 75,000 tons of ammunition, and 162,000 tons of petrol behind. If the nation was to fight on, some way had to be found to make good these huge losses and, clearly it could not be done by British industry alone. The government turned to the Commonwealth and to the USA for help.

At that time, the US Army had just 464 tanks, most of which were of the light pattern. Perhaps with one nervous eye on the events that had unfolded in Europe during May and June 1940, the American National Munitions Program had standardised on the M2A4 light tank and the M2A1 medium, with 365 units of the light tank ordered, and 2,000 of the medium. At the same time, representatives of the British Tank Commission arrived in the USA in June 1940 with the intention of buying medium tanks and, by April 1941, American Locomotive, General Motors and Baldwin Locomotive had all produced pilot models for the M3 medium tank and production was in full swing by August.

In early 1941, a small batch of M2 light tanks came to Britain for training and, by July of that year, the first examples of the improved M3 light tank arrived and were promptly shipped to Egypt. The first M3 medium tanks, known both as the General Lee and the General Grant, according to configuration, followed in 1942. By the time the war was over, the US government had supplied tanks and tank parts worth a total of $3.55 billion to the Allies under the Lend-Lease Act of 1941. Britain's share of this huge figure consisted of 25,554 tanks – made up of 5,473 M3/M5 Stuart light tanks, 2,900 M3 Lee/Grant medium tanks, and 17,181 M4 Sherman medium tanks.

M3/M5 Light Tank – Stuart

Before the Second World War, the US Army shared the British view that tanks should be classified as light, medium and heavy. In the light category, the Ordnance Board had standardised on the M2, which had been developed by the Tank Design Department at Rock Island Arsenal. It went into production as the M2A4 in April 1940, with just 375 vehicles constructed. However, having seen the German tanks in operation in Poland, it was apparent that the M2 was scarcely adequate, and work was instigated to improve the armour. Unfortunately, the increased weight compromised the ride quality and the engineers were forced to redesign the suspension system, repositioning the rear track idler to increase the effective track length. The design of what had now become the M3 was standardised in July 1940 and went into production in March 1941. Although scarcely at the cutting edge of tank design, the 37mm gun was at least a nominal match for the original 37mm *KwK L/46.5* weapon of the German Panzer III, and the tank was relatively fast, being capable of 36mph on roads and around 20mph across country.

The compact, high-sided boxy hull was of riveted construction, measuring 179in in length and 88in in width; with a 51mm maximum thickness of armour. This gave a combat weight of 12.25 tons. The seven-sided turret had a separate commander's cupola, and was also of riveted construction, mounting the American 37mm M5 or M6 gun. Three .30in Browning machine guns were also mounted in the turret, with two more in side sponsons. A small number of machines were fitted with a 220bhp Guiberson Buda Model T-1020-4 nine-cylinder radial air-cooled diesel engine of 16,731cc, but most were powered by a Continental W670-9A seven-cylinder radial petrol engine producing 242bhp from 10,946cc. Drive was conveyed to the front sprockets via a five-speed manual transmission.

In August 1941, the M3A1 variant was standardised, dispensing with the cupola in favour of a turret basket, with the original turret replaced by a welded design with power traverse and a gyrostabiliser. Improvements were also made to the gun mount, which included fitting two periscopes, and the sponson-mounted machine guns were omitted. The weight was increased to 12.75 tons. The British referred to this variant as the Stuart III or Stuart IV, according to the type of engine.

Production of the original M3 ended in February 1943, after a total of 4,621 had been built, with both versions being declared obsolete in July.

A temporary shortage of radial engines led to the development of the M3E2 and M3E3 pilot models, powered by twin Cadillac Series 42 V8 petrol engines, producing 125bhp each from 5,670cc. The engines were coupled to a GM

Hydramatic automatic transmission with six forward speeds and two reverse. Other improvements included changes to the hull, which was now of welded construction with a cast, rounded front, providing more space in the four-man crew compartment.

It had also been planned that there would be a welded-hull variant of the M3A1, which would have been designated M3A2, but there was no series production, and the next round of modifications resulted in the M3A3, known as the Stuart V by the British. This was standardised in August 1942. Weighing 14 tons, the M3A3 included a radio bustle at the back of the turret and had three additional periscopes; the gun mount was redesigned to incorporate a telescope; and there was better armoured protection for the driver. The sponsons were extended to house additional fuel-storage tanks and provide ammunition stowage, and sand shields were fitted over the suspension units. Improvements were also made to the crew's facilities, including redesigned steering gear, a detachable windshield, and better fire protection. The M3A3 was produced only with the Continental engine, and was reclassified 'limited standard' in April 1943, meaning that it met certain criteria set by the US Ordnance Department but did not reach the required standard to be issued to combat units.

M3 light tanks were constructed by American Car and Foundry, with 5,811 vehicles built. Production ceased in August 1942.

At the end of 1941 Cadillac started to build tanks at plants in Detroit, Michigan and Southgate, California and one of the first vehicles on the assembly lines was a production version of the M3E2/M3E3, intended to replace the M3. To avoid confusion with the M4 medium tanks, the new model was redesignated M5. It was similar in design to the M3E2/M3E3 but had a maximum armour thickness of 67mm, putting the weight up to 14.75 tons, and incorporated a six-speed automatic transmission with a two-speed auxiliary unit. The M5 was standardised in February 1942, but was reclassified 'limited standard' in April 1943.

In September 1942, the M5 was replaced by the M5A1, with a lengthened turret similar to that fitted to the earlier M3A3, a new gun mount and a driver's escape hatch. The anti-aircraft gun mount was repositioned to the right, and the internal arrangements of the hull and turret were rearranged to provide more space for the crew. The battle weight was now 15.15 tons. The M5A1 was downgraded to 'substitute standard' in July 1944, meaning that it was authorised for issue in lieu of a 'standard' item of like nature and quality.

The M5, or Stuart VI, was not supplied in large numbers to Britain, but a few served in northwest Europe in 1944. Production of the M5 was undertaken by American Car and Foundry, Cadillac and Massey-Harris. Between them these manufacturers constructed 8,884 vehicles, of which 2,074 were M5s and 6,810 were M5A1s. Production was terminated in October 1944.

M3 Medium Tank – Lee/Grant

The M3 medium tank was a logical development of the T5, which had appeared in mock-up form in 1937. A year later, a fully armoured prototype had been constructed, mounting a 37mm gun, and was put through its paces at Aberdeen Proving Ground. With minor refinements the T5 was standardised as the M2 medium tank and was put into production at the Rock Island Arsenal in Illinois but, after just eighteen units had been built, it was superseded by the up-armoured and improved M2A1. The original plan had been to build 1,000 M2A1s, but the production facilities at Rock Island were modest and by 15 August 1940 Chrysler had agreed to build the M2A1 in a new government-financed, purpose-built tank arsenal in Detroit.

However, the 37mm gun of the M2A1 was insufficiently powerful to take on the more modern German tanks and, after just ninety-four had been built, the production contract was cancelled. Almost immediately, Rock Island Arsenal started work on designing a new medium tank, designated M3, which would be armed with a 75mm gun. With just sixty days for the design work, there was little choice but to produce an up-armoured, up-gunned version of the M2A1, though the basic hull and the Wright Continental air-cooled radial engine and running gear were retained, as was the vertical volute spring suspension (VVSS). The major challenge was how to accommodate the big 75mm M2/M3 howitzer – with no access to a suitable turret ring, the gun ended up mounted in a sponson on the right-hand side of the hull. There was also a revolving turret mounting a 37mm M5/M6 gun, and on top of this was the commander's cupola, mounting a .30in machine gun – looking for all the world like another turret.

The original M3, M3A4 and M3A5 variants had a riveted hull designed for a crew of six; the hull of the M3A1 variant was of cast construction, whilst the M3A2 and M3A3 were welded. For most variants, the hull width was 123in and the length 222in; the M3A4 was 236in long. The maximum thickness of armour was 57mm on the turret and 50mm on the hull, and the combat weight varied between 26.75 and 28.6 tons according to the method of manufacture and the power unit.

In its original guise, and in the subsequent M3A1 and M3A2 versions, the M3 was powered by a rear-mounted Wright Continental R-975-C1 or EC2 nine-cylinder air-cooled radial petrol engine producing 340bhp from a capacity of 15,945cc. The M3A3 and M3A5 variants were fitted with twin General Motors 6-71 diesel engines, each producing 205bhp from 13,930cc, whilst the Chrysler WC multi-bank unit went into the M3A4, incorporating five six-cylinder blocks disposed around a single crankcase to give 425bhp from 20,533cc. A shortage of Wright radial engines also led to the limited production of the M3(D) and M3A1(D) variants, which were fitted with a 220bhp Guiberson Buda Model T-1020-4 nine-cylinder radial air-cooled diesel engine of 16,731cc. In all cases, the tracks were driven by the front sprockets through a five-speed manual transmission.

Production started in April 1941 and, alongside the initial 1,000 tanks constructed for the US Army, the British Purchasing Committee placed orders for a further 1,686 units – 500 from the Pullman Standard Car Company, 501 from either the Lima Locomotive Works or the Pressed Steel Car Company, and 685 from Baldwin Locomotive. The US Lend-Lease Act had yet to be passed and these tanks were supplied on a 'cash and carry' basis. The British were not entirely happy with some features of the design, and the British version was fitted with a larger cast turret, lacking the cupola but designed to accommodate a Number 19 radio set in a bustle. The British dubbed 'their' version 'General Grant' and the US Army version 'General Lee', although the word 'General' was soon dropped. The original M3 was described as Grant I, and the M3A5 was Grant II; the US pattern M3 was known as Lee I, the M3A1 was Lee II, the M3A2 was Lee III (although none of these was supplied to the British), the M3A3 was Lee IV, the M3A1(D) was Lee V and the M3A4 was known as Lee VI.

Obsolete M3s were also converted for a variety of roles including artillery prime mover, mine-clearance vehicle, searchlight carrier, flame-thrower, armoured recovery vehicle, command vehicle, etc. The chassis was also used as for the T24 3in gun motor carriage, and the M7 105mm howitzer motor carriage; when these became redundant some were converted to Kangaroo armoured personnel carriers.

With its 75mm main gun, heavy armour and excellent reliability, the M3 out-classed most of the British tanks of the period and was able to engage the early German tanks and anti-tank guns on a relatively equal basis. Top speed was around 26mph on roads, reducing to 16mph across country.

M4 Medium Tank – Sherman

The M4 Sherman medium tank is probably the best known Allied tank of the Second World War. It served with the US Army and Marine Corps, the British Army, the British Commonwealth Armies, the Soviet Union, the Free French, the Polish government-in-exile, Brazil and China.

Work on the M4 medium tank – it was the British who dubbed it the 'General Sherman', or more usually just Sherman – started almost as soon as the M3 medium had gone into production. Although far from perfect, the design was enormously successful and remained in production from late 1941 to the end of the war. Whilst not the best protected tank of the conflict, nor the hardest hitting (particularly with the original 75mm gun), it was simple to build, reliable and easy to maintain – and, above all, it was available in large numbers.

The drawings and specification of what was at first known as the T6 medium tank were signed off at Aberdeen Proving Ground on 18 April 1941, with five different schemes suggested. The simplest of these utilised the lower hull of the M3 along with the engine, transmission and running gear. Both cast and welded upper hulls were proposed, designed for a crew of five, and mounting a new cast turret with the 75mm M3 gun. A wooden mock-up was produced in May 1941 for the approval of the Armored Force Board, and a pilot model, with a cast distinctively rounded hull was completed in September 1941. As with the earlier M3, the engine was the Wright Continental R-975-C1 nine-cylinder air-cooled radial unit, producing 400bhp from 15,945cc, and coupled to a five-speed manual gearbox driving the front sprockets.

In October 1941, the M4 was standardised, with production planned at eleven plants, including those already producing the M3. The first production units were of the cast-hull M4A1 configuration starting in February 1942 at the Lima Locomotive Works in Lima, Ohio, under British Ministry of Supply contract. Known by the British as the Sherman I, this tank saw its first action with the 8th Army at El Alamein in October 1942.

The Sherman was constantly under development, often more to expedite production rather than to improve the breed. For example, whilst the hull of the original M4 and of the A2, A3, A4, A5 and A6 was of welded construction, the M4A1 had a cast hull, which tended to make the interior rather cramped. Similarly, although the Wright Continental was fitted into the M4 and the M4A1, there were also other engine configurations: twin GM 6-71 diesel engines, each of 13,930cc, with a combined power output of 410bhp, were fitted to the M4A2; a 500bhp Ford V8 GAA petrol engine of 18,026cc was used in the M4A3; the Chrysler WC multi-bank unit, incorporating five six-cylinder blocks disposed around a single crankcase to give 425bhp from 20,533cc, was fitted into the M4A4; and a 450bhp Caterpillar RD-1820 radial diesel was installed in the M4A6.

The suspension, initially employing vertical volute springs, was redesigned, with the springs placed horizontally. This horizontal volute spring suspension (HVSS) resulted in an improved ride and extended the life of the suspension units. It also meant that the suspension was better able to accommodate the increasing weight of later vehicle designs.

Compared to other tank designs of the period, the M4 presented a rather high profile, with a maximum height of 117in, although this was a considerable improvement on the M3 Lee/Grant. The hull was 232–288in long, according to the variant, and 103–106in wide, with the later horizontal volute spring suspension increasing this latter figure to 120in. The maximum thickness of armour was 75mm on the turret and 50–62mm on the hull, again depending on the variant, giving an all-up battle weight in the order of 29.7 to 32.5 tons. Maximum speed was in the order of 24–29mph on the road and 15–20mph across country, although it was a bumpy ride and the tank also exhibited an unpleasant tendency to catch fire when hit, giving rise to its 'Ronson' nickname.

The most serious drawback of the Sherman was the main gun and, as the war progressed, it was increasingly outclassed. With the original 75mm M3 gun, the Sherman could not defeat either a Panther or a Tiger on equal terms. In 1944, the 75mm weapon was replaced by the 76mm M1 anti-tank gun. This offered some improvements in performance but the more powerful German guns could still penetrate the Sherman's frontal armour, whilst the Sherman had little chance of defeating a Panther or a Tiger unless it could shoot it from the side or the rear, where the armour was thinner. When the British 17-pounder (76.2mm) gun was fitted into the Sherman Firefly in 1943/44, the M4 was finally almost a match for the heavier German tanks.

A total of 17,181 Shermans were supplied to Britain. The original M4 was designated Sherman I, whilst subsequent variants were identified as Sherman II through Sherman VII, with the Firefly being designated Sherman VC.

The M4 chassis was also used for the M7 105mm gun motor carriage, and was widely adapted by both the British and US armies to a wide range of specialised roles, including flame-thrower, armoured recovery vehicle, tank 'dozer, rocket launcher and a range of mine-clearance devices.

The first examples of the M3 entered Britain in July 1941. Officially named General Stuart by the British Army, and simply referred to as the Stuart, it saw its first action in Libya in November 1941. *(IWM, H17289)*

The British Army referred to the petrol-engined version as Stuart I, whilst the diesel was Stuart II; both shared the same riveted form of construction. *(Tank Museum)*

In recognition of its excellent reliability and general ease of operation, the British crews dubbed the M3 'Honey'. This example wears sand skirts over the tracks. *(Warehouse Collection)*

The Lee/Grant was an ungainly machine, 123in high, which meant that it tended to stick out like the proverbial sore thumb – by contrast the German Panzer III was just 96in high. The designers were also well aware that the sponson-mounted gun was a compromise that would often require the tank to be manoeuvred into the right position to achieve the required aim. *(Warehouse Collection)*

The M3 first saw action at the Battle of Gazala in North Africa against Rommel on 27 May 1941. When the M3 was superseded by the M4 Sherman, British M3s were shipped to Burma and to Australia. The photograph shows the US Army's M3 Lee with the commander's cupola. *(Warehouse Collection)*

The major disadvantage of the Lee/Grant was its height, though the riveted hull of the early versions was also a drawback, since the rivets had a nasty habit of breaking loose under fire and ricocheting around the crew compartment – but this was equally true of many contemporary British tanks. (*Warehouse Collection*)

The British version, known as the Grant, was fitted with a larger cast turret, lacking the cupola but designed to accommodate a Number 19 radio set in a bustle. (*Tank Museum*)

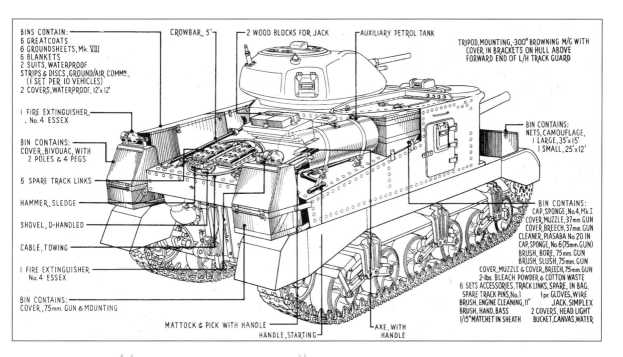

BINS CONTAIN:-
6 GREATCOATS
6 GROUNDSHEETS, Mk. VIII
6 BLANKETS
2 SUITS, WATERPROOF
STRIPS & DISCS, GROUND/AIR COMMN.,
(I SET PER IO VEHICLES)
2 COVERS, WATERPROOF, 12'x 12'

I FIRE EXTINGUISHER,
. No. 4 ESSEX

BIN CONTAINS:
COVER, BIVOUAC, WITH
2 POLES & 4 PEGS

6 SPARE TRACK LINKS

HAMMER, SLEDGE

SHOVEL, D-HANDLED

CABLE, TOWING

I FIRE EXTINGUISHER
No. 4 ESSEX

BIN CONTAINS:-
COVER, 75mm. GUN & MOUNTING

CROWBAR, 5'

2 WOOD BLOCKS FOR JACK

AUXILIARY PETROL TANK

TRIPOD, MOUNTING, ·300" BROWNING M/G WITH
COVER IN BRACKETS ON HULL ABOVE
FORWARD END OF L/H TRACK GUARD

BIN CONTAINS:
NETS, CAMOUFLAGE,
I LARGE, 35'x 15'
I SMALL, 25'x 12'

BIN CONTAINS:
CAP, SPONGE, No. 4, Mk. I
COVER, MUZZLE, 37mm. GUN
COVER, BREECH, 37mm. GUN
CLEANER, PIASABA No. 20 IN
CAP, SPONGE, No. 6 (75mm. GUN)
BRUSH, BORE, 75mm. GUN
BRUSH, SLUSH, 75mm. GUN
COVER, MUZZLE & COVER, BREECH, 75mm. GUN
2-lbs. BLEACH POWDER & COTTON WASTE
6 SETS ACCESSORIES, TRACK LINKS, SPARE, IN BAG,
SPARE TRACK PINS, No. I   I pr. GLOVES, WIRE
BRUSH, ENGINE CLEANING, II"   JACK, SIMPLEX
BRUSH, HAND, BASS   2 COVERS, HEAD LIGHT
I/15"MATCHET IN SHEATH   BUCKET, CANVAS, WATER

MATTOCK & PICK WITH HANDLE

HANDLE, STARTING

AXE, WITH
HANDLE

External rear stowage diagram for the British Grant. *(Warehouse Collection)*

A total of 6,258 M3 tanks were produced, most of them (4,924) of the original M3 pattern. Of these, 2,855 were supplied to the British Army, and 1,368 went to the Soviet Union. *(IWM, H21027)*

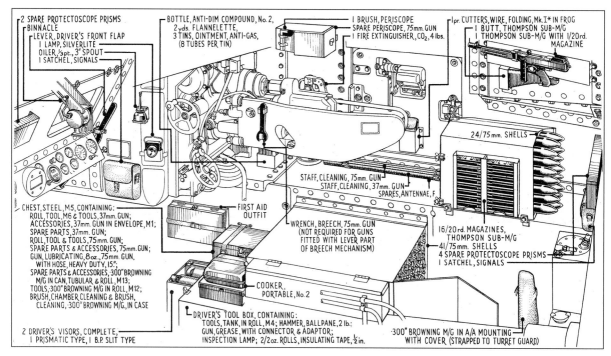

Stowage diagram for the Grant fighting compartment. *(Warehouse Collection)*

The M3 was never intended to be anything more than a compromise, whilst the designers tried to find a way to mount the 75mm gun in a proper revolving turret. *(Warehouse Collection)*

Despite its shortcomings, the M3 went into production at the Detroit Tank Arsenal, and at the American Locomotive Company (ALCO) and the Baldwin Locomotive Works during April 1941 just three weeks after the final drawings were produced. Tanks intended for Britain were produced by Baldwin Locomotive Works, as well as by Pressed Steel, Pullman Standard, and Lima Locomotive Works. *(Warehouse Collection)*

The detailed design characteristics for the M4 Sherman had been prepared by the US Army Ordnance Department by the end of August 1940 with the intention of producing a fast, dependable tank that would improve on the stop-gap M3, and which would be capable of defeating any of the Axis tanks – effectively meaning the later incarnations of the Panzer III. *(Warehouse Collection)*

During the conflict, US factories produced a total of almost 50,000 Shermans, compared to a grand total of 48,456 German tanks of all types produced during 1939–45. *(Warehouse Collection)*

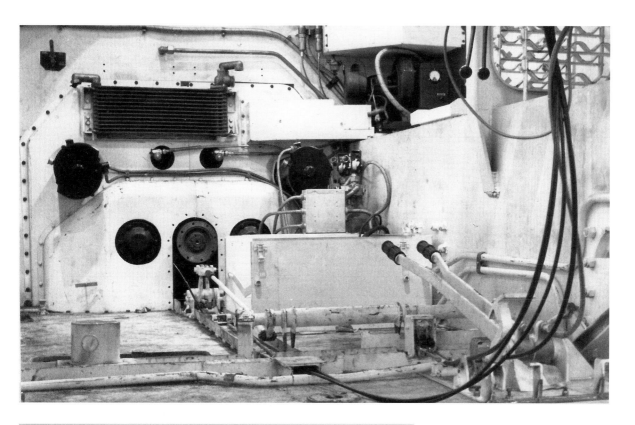

The Sherman driving compartment. *(Warehouse Collection)*

This unusual low-level view shows the cast hull and the massive three-piece bolted nose of the M4A4. *(Warehouse Collection)*

British tank crew in Normandy effecting repairs to a Sherman which has been damaged by a German 88mm shell. *(IWM, B5423)*

M4, M4A1 and M4A5 Shermans were all fitted with a Wright or Continental radial engine. This example belongs to the US Army. (*Tank Museum*)

Late production M4A2 with one-piece cast nose and M34A1 mount for the 75mm gun. (*Warehouse Collection*)

It was not until the British quick-firing 17-pounder (76.2mm) was fitted into the Sherman Firefly in 1943/44 that the M4 was able to take on the heavier German tanks on a more equal basis. *(Warehouse Collection)*

The Sherman was certainly the most significant tank operated by the British Army and saw more widespread use than any of the comparable British designs during the conflict. This is the Firefly VC. *(Tank Museum)*

Simultaneous facing and drilling of the cast turret for the M4 at the Detroit Tank Arsenal. *(Warehouse Collection)*

The M4A2 was fitted with twin GM 6-71 diesel engines, and most vehicles were supplied for Lend-Lease. *(Warehouse Collection)*

Produced by the Dunlop Rubber Company and RFD of Godalming, this inflatable dummy Sherman tank was designed to deceive enemy aircraft regarding the numbers and deployment of Allied tanks. *(IWM, H42532)*

Chapter Seven

Specials, Engineers' Tanks and 'Funnies'

So-called 'special tanks' started to appear as early as 1917 when the British Army modified Mk IV heavy tanks, equipping them with fascine bundles or hollow timber cylinders to allow ditches to be crossed. Both Mk IV and Mk V tanks were also fitted with hinged ramps which provided a means of crossing other obstacles – thus, creating the first bridging tanks. Others had their armaments removed and were adapted for use as supply vehicles or gun carriers, whilst the armoured recovery vehicle was developed by the simple expedient of attaching a jib and pulley block or powered crane to the front of an obsolete tank. Flame-thrower tanks were discussed, although never produced in the First World War.

In 1918, after the Armistice, the development impetus was lost and few special tanks saw service during the interwar years. The outbreak of the Second World War saw a resurgence of interest in using armoured vehicles for specialised roles, including anti-aircraft defence, mine clearing, bridging, etc.; in the lead-up to the D-Day landings, a range of so-called 'funnies' was developed, each tasked with overcoming a particular problem. These vehicles made an enormous contribution to the success of the landings.

Anti-Aircraft Tanks

In the immediate pre-war years, the British Army had tended to favour mounting anti-aircraft weapons on 15cwt trucks, initially using the *portée* method in which the gun was intended to be dismounted before use, but latterly using gun carriers from which the gun could be fired without dismounting.

From mid-1943, the Germans had started to mount heavier anti-aircraft guns on the chassis of the *PzKpfw III* and *PzKpfw IV* tanks, and the British soon followed suit, with the Crusader III adapted to mount either a single Bofors 40mm anti-aircraft gun in a tall, square turret (Crusader III, AA, Mk I), or latterly, twin Oerlikon 20mm cannon (Crusader III, AA, Mk II) in a lower-profile turret. A Mk III variant had the radio equipment moved from the turret into the hull, and a few vehicles were also equipped with triple Oerlikon cannon in an open mount, for training purposes.

Centaur chassis were also fitted for anti-aircraft use, initially using Polsten cannon (Centaur, AA, Mk I), but subsequently with the same turret as the Crusader, mounting two Oerlikon 20mm cannon (Centaur, AA, Mk II).

Although intended for use during the Normandy landings, Allied air superiority was such that the vehicles were not required and the anti-aircraft units were disbanded shortly after June 1944.

Armoured Recovery Vehicles

Given the size and weight of even the average tank of the period, compared to the average wheeled heavy recovery vehicle, it should have been self-evident that the most suitable vehicle for recovering a disabled tank was another tank. Yet it was not until February 1942 that the British Army began to look into the question of converting tanks to the role of armoured recovery vehicles (ARV). The Royal Electrical and Mechanical Engineers (REME) workshops at Arborfield produced experimental ARVs based on the Covenanter, Crusader, Churchill and Grant chassis, largely by the simple expedient of removing the turret and gun and equipping the hull with basic recovery equipment.

The Crusader and Covenanter were both rejected as being unsuitable, but, with their comparatively roomy hulls, the Churchill and Grant were both considered for further development, appearing as the Churchill ARV Mk I, and the Grant ARV Mk I. A 3-ton jib was stowed on the rear of the hull: it was designed to be erected at the front or rear as required, and could be used to remove and replace a tank engine and/or gearbox. The jib could similarly recover a disabled or bogged-down tank. Cavalier, Centaur and Sherman hulls were also adapted in much the same way.

In 1943, the British Army started to receive the US Army's T2 tank recovery vehicle. Based on the M3 Lee hull, the T2 was equipped with a high-lift jib and a heavy winch, and led to the development of a similarly equipped British vehicle, designed by the REME workshops and constructed using both Sherman and Churchill hulls. Known as the ARV Mk II, a fixed turret was installed, mounting a dummy gun, and providing space for a Croft 60-ton winch. There was a detachable 3.5-ton winch at the front, and a fixed 9.5-ton winch at the rear, as well as a substantial earth anchor. The British Army also used the Sherman-based M32 tank recovery vehicle, describing it as the ARV Mk III.

Mention should also be made of the beach armoured recovery vehicles (BARV) developed specifically for recovering drowned or disabled tanks from the D-Day beaches. Designed by REME, and constructed using both Churchill and Sherman hulls, the BARV had the turret and gun removed and the hull sides raised to allow the vehicle to wade in up to eight feet of water. The Churchill version never progressed beyond the prototype stage.

Assault Vehicle, Royal Engineers

After the unsuccessful assault at Dieppe in August 1942, Lieutenant-Colonel J. J. Donovan of the Royal Canadian Engineers suggested that such operations might have a greater degree of success if a form of tank could be developed that would carry the sappers and their equipment, as well as providing a sufficient degree of protection to allow working under fire. By December 1942, a prototype had been constructed and successfully demonstrated by the Royal Canadian Engineers, using a Churchill II. The interior of the hull was cleared of unnecessary fittings, and stowage compartments were provided for the engineers' equipment. A 290mm *Pétard* spigot mortar was installed in the turret, capable of firing a 40lb 'dustbin' charge 230 yards. A second prototype was constructed soon afterwards using a Churchill III, although lacking the mortar.

Designated assault vehicle, Royal Engineers (AVRE), the first 108 vehicles were constructed by the workshops of the Royal Electrical and Mechanical Engineers (REME). Although not all were equipped with the mortar, the AVRE was used to equip 1st Assault Brigade of the 79th Armoured Division in time for use on the D-Day beaches. MG Cars Limited was subsequently given a contract for adapting a further 574 Churchill III and IV tanks to AVRE configuration.

The AVRE was a very adaptable vehicle, with brackets on the front and sides of the hull to accept all kinds of attachments. These included the 30-foot-span small box-girder bridge (SBG); various hessian and canvas mat-laying devices, including the tank landing craft (TLC) laying devices – the Bobbin Carpet, Twin Bobbin Carpet, Roly Poly, and Log Carpet, all designed to prevent tanks from becoming bogged down in soft ground; the Onion and Goat demolition-charge placing devices, although only the Goat was produced in quantity; and the fascine, a bundle of 8-foot long wooden stakes, which was used as an aid to crossing ditches and trenches. AVREs were also used to push 'skid' Bailey bridges into position.

There were also experiments with improving the firepower of the mortar. The Woodpecker mounted four 290mm mortars on the hull sides, whilst Ardeer Aggie was fitted with a recoilless mortar, which fired a 54lb projectile 450 yards. Experiments with Shermans as the basis for an AVRE were subsequently abandoned, although the Canadian Army did convert the M3-based Ram tank.

Bridgelayers

Following the end of the First World War there had been experiments using Mk V** heavy tanks as bridging vehicles. During the interwar years, there were further experiments with Dragon Mk I field artillery tractors as bridge carriers. By 1925, a 16-foot-span light-girder bridge had been designed for use with the Vickers medium tank – although fine in principle, it was found that the span was too short to be of practical use. Subsequently, Matilda infantry tanks were used to push bridge sections across gaps of up to 80 feet, and Churchills were similarly used with 'skid' Bailey bridges during the Second World War.

However, most bridgelayers of the period were designed actually to carry the bridge and to launch it across the gap. Work on bridgelaying tanks had started in the mid-1930s, when Covenanters and Valentines were converted to the bridgelayer role using a hydraulically deployed scissors bridge known as 'scissors bridge, 30 foot, number 1'.

With the introduction of the much heavier Churchill tank, the original scissors bridge was no longer adequate and a new rigid-span 30-foot bridge was developed – described as 'bridge, tank, 30 foot, number 2' – to be carried on the hull of the Churchill IV. The bridge was launched from the hull of the tank but lacked the central pivot, simply needing to be rotated through 180 degrees. Churchill bridgelayers were used in Italy and in northwest Europe.

Churchill and Sherman tanks were also used as the basis of the armoured ramp carrier – generally known as Ark. Ramps were attached to either end of the hull, and a trackway was fitted to the top of the hull: in operation, the tank was driven into the centre of the ditch or trench, or up against a sea wall, and the ramps were folded out at either end to form a continuous bridge, with the tank remaining in the ditch during use. The Churchill Ark I had a span of 28 feet, whilst the Ark II had a span of 48 to 54 feet, according to the types of ramp fitted. Arks were used in Italy and northwest Europe.

CDL Searchlight Tanks

Some experiments with searchlight-equipped tanks had taken place during the closing months of the First World War, presumably in an effort to allow combat to continue into the hours of darkness, but it was not until the years leading up to the Second World War that anyone came up with the idea of using powerful searchlights as a weapon, effectively to paralyse the opposition. In 1937, a searchlight weapon was demonstrated to the War Office, with further trials at the Royal Armoured Corps Gunnery School at Lulworth in Dorset, in June 1940.

Following the success of these trials, the Vulcan Foundry and the Ashford works of the Southern Railway Company were given a contract for 300 turrets, each equipped with a 12.75 million-candela carbon-arc searchlight powered by a generator driven by the tank's engine. Described as the canal defence light (CDL), these turrets were mounted on the Matilda infantry tank. The light was reflected from a huge parabolic mirror and focused through a lens, emerging through a vertical slit, covered by a movable shutter, on the turret front. The slit could be rapidly opened and closed, creating a stroboscopic effect designed to dazzle, disorientate and temporarily blind the enemy. It was proposed that CDL tanks could be used in pairs, deployed at some distance apart, with their searchlight beams focused on an enemy stronghold, which would allow infantry to advance, unseen in the darkness between the two vehicles.

Three British regiments were equipped with CDL Matildas and Churchills, and latterly with M3 Lee/Grants, where a separate engine was provided to drive the generator. The US Army also raised a number of CDL battalions, three of which went to France some time after D-Day. During the Rhine crossing in March 1945, both British and American CDL tanks were stationed on the riverbank, scanning the water with their searchlights to illuminate possible enemy sabotage teams attempting to blow the bridge.

Duplex-Drive Amphibious Tanks

Amphibious tanks had been tested during the First World War, but none had worked well enough to be used in combat. Nevertheless, development continued during the interwar years, with small tanks that had natural buoyancy, or with conventional vehicles carrying flotation devices. In June 1941, the prolific Hungarian inventor, Nicholas Straussler, finally solved the problem of making tanks float by using a folding canvas screen attached to a frame welded around the top of the hull. The screen was raised by compressed air – a process that took around fifteen minutes – and was secured by stays. By increasing the displacement of the hull, this allowed the tank to float. A second drive system, which diverted power from the tracks to rear-mounted propellers, allowed the tanks to 'swim' from landing craft to beach – and also gave them their name of duplex drive, or DD, the name having been chosen to obscure the role of the vehicle. In the water, the tanks were steered by means of a rudder and by swivelling the propellers on a horizontal axis.

Major General Percy Hobart of the 79th Armoured Division took the principle of Straussler's folding screen and carried out trials in Portsmouth Harbour using a modified Tetrarch. At the same time, a Crusader was fitted with inflatable pontoons for comparison. The success of the Tetrarch led to the selection of the Valentine as the basis for the development of the duplex-drive tank, with the development work given to the Metropolitan-Cammell. Plans were also put in hand to convert Sherman, and even Cromwell and Churchill tanks, for the amphibious role.

Deliveries of the Valentines were completed by the beginning of 1944. By this time, the DD tanks had already been issued to units for training purposes, and the majority of the American, British and Canadian DD tank crews did their preliminary training using Valentines. However, it soon became clear that the Sherman was more suitable for amphibious use, and the conversion was carried out using Sherman III and Sherman V variants. The modifications were similar to those made to the Valentine, but the increased weight of the Sherman dictated an increase in the height of the canvas screen. Drive to the propellers was taken from the rear sprockets using bevel gears, with the advantage that the tracks were running as soon as the tank touched the beach. The propellers were designed to hinge upwards when not in use.

DD Shermans were used very effectively on D-Day, although rough seas could, and did, drive the vehicles off course. The Shermans were also used during the Rhine crossing in 1945 and a small number of Valentine DDs were used in Italy in 1945.

Flame-Thrower Tanks

In July 1940, Lagonda Motors constructed and demonstrated a portable flame-thrower device, with a range of little more than 100 feet, to the Department of Miscellaneous Weapons Development (DMWD). The weapon came to the attention of Major General Sir Donald Banks, Director-General of the Petroleum Warfare Department, and he asked Lagonda if a larger mobile unit could be designed with a range of 150 feet or more. Eventually, Lagonda managed to produce a unit that could pump burning petroleum fuel 350 feet.

Although indisputably a fearsome weapon, at the time it seems that it had no clear application until it was suggested that there might be a role in the protection of shipping against low-level attack, and that it could be equally effective in defending airfields. An initial order was placed by the Admiralty, for what was described as the Mk I vertical flame-thrower, intended to be used from the decks of ships.

However, the flame-thrower became better known as a vehicle-mounted weapon following Lagonda's development of an experimental armoured vehicle using a Commer truck chassis. This led to the production of what was known as the Cockatrice. The first of these, the 'light Cockatrice', used a Bedford QL 3-ton 4x4 chassis, whilst the 'heavy Cockatrice' was mounted on the 6x6 AEC Model O854 chassis. The equipment fitted to the Cockatrice was subsequently adapted by the Canadian Army for use on the universal carrier, in which form it was described as the 'Ronson' flame-thrower, and this, in turn, led to the development of the Wasp. At the end of July 1942 work started on adapting the Wasp to allow it to be fitted to tanks.

Early development work was carried out on a pair of Valentines, one using a projector ignited by cordite charges, the other operated by gas pressure. The fuel was carried in a trailer and the flame projector was mounted on the hull front. Trials showed that the gas-operated system was better and this led to the development of what became known as the Churchill Crocodile.

A dozen pilot models were ordered before the War Office decided that the Churchill lacked sufficient protection for what would, inevitably, be combat at close quarters, and that a smaller, more mobile vehicle might be better. Nevertheless, work on the Crocodile continued, under the direction of R. P. Fraser of Lagonda, and a prototype towing a special gas-pressurised 400-gallon fuel trailer was demonstrated in January 1943. The fuel was passed to the towing vehicle under pressure through a special articulated coupling, and was ejected through a projector nozzle fitted into the front of the hull. Early examples used the original long-barrelled Wasp Mk I projector, but this was subsequently superseded by the Wasp Mk II, which was capable of emitting burning fuel at a rate of more than six gallons a second. The major advantage was that the flamer-thrower equipment did not require the main gun to be removed and, although the trailer impaired the mobility of the tank to some degree, it could be jettisoned once empty and the vehicle could resume its previous role as a gun tank.

Lagonda became the parent firm of a group of companies described as the 'Crocodile Production Group' and some 800 (out of a contracted 1,000) Crocodiles were constructed. Initial work concentrated on the Churchill IV, but production vehicles used the Churchill VII chassis.

The Matilda Frog was similarly equipped, and there were examples of experimental flame-thrower Shermans under the names Salamander and Adder. Canadian Ram tanks were also equipped as flame-throwers, when they were known as the Ram Badger.

The Crocodile proved enormously effective against pillboxes and strong points and was deployed in Italy and then, in quantity, from D-Day onwards.

Mine-clearing Tanks

During the Second World War, huge numbers of anti-tank mines were laid by the opposing armies, as well as even greater numbers of anti-personnel, or land mines. Although many were laid in the Soviet Union, there was, nevertheless, considerable concern amongst those planning the invasion of north-west Europe regarding the dangers that the mines presented to the advancing armies. All kinds of solutions to the problem were proposed, including explosive devices, flails, rollers and ploughs – all of them attached to modified tank hulls. Many were immediately dismissed as being impractical, but others were developed to the point where they became quite successful.

Explosive devices

Various attempts were made to develop devices that could clear a lane through a minefield by exploding the mines ahead of an advancing tank. Two such devices, dubbed Snake and Conger, consisted of a long hosepipe or cylinder of explosive that could be pushed across a minefield and detonated remotely. It was found that the Snake could clear a path about 30in wide, certainly sufficient to allow infantry to pass through safely. Subsequently there were trials with rocket-propelled Snakes fired from multiple tubes mounted on the hull of a Churchill, but, despite some limited production, the rocket-propelled Snakes were never deployed in anger.

A similar device was dubbed Tapeworm. Designed to be towed across the minefield by a flail tank, Tapeworm consisted of a flexible hosepipe that could be filled with liquid explosive once in position and then detonated.

Flails

Development of the flail tank dates back to 1939 when the Mechanization Board proposed that anti-tank mines could be exploded by weights attached to the ends of spring-steel strips on a revolving drum carried ahead of a tank. However, it was not until the summer of 1941, when the problem of anti-tank mines in North Africa had become acute, that serious consideration was given to the deployment of a flail tank. Major Du Toit of the South African Forces suggested replacing the spring-steel strips and weights with revolving chains and, by November 1941, Du Toit was with AEC at Southall working on the development of a practical flail.

Initially described as the 'tank winch', but retrospectively known as the Baron Mk I, the first prototype mounted the flail onto a Matilda II, still with its turret and gun. A cross-shaft, fitted with two rows of chains, was carried on arms at the front of the tank about six feet above the ground. The shaft could be raised or lowered hydraulically, and was driven at about 80rpm by a Chrysler petrol engine. The device was intended to flail mines, cut through barbed wire, and destroy anti-tank earthworks, but trials showed that the engine was not sufficiently powerful, nor could the rotor be held at a constant height. The Baron Mk II appeared in April 1942, using a six-cylinder Bedford engine to power the rotor and the hydraulic raising and lowering system. The length and arrangement of the chains was varied to give a consistent beat pattern whilst minimising damage to the chains. It was found that barbed wire became entangled around the flail rotor, occasionally jamming it solid, and the rotor was eventually fitted with circular saw blades and V-notch wire cutters.

Clearly, the device had considerable potential, but more power was required to drive the chains at a higher speed. Earlier experiments with a 'perambulator' device that used a Matilda tank to push a flail were abandoned, and work started on the Baron Mk IIIA.

The turret and gun of the Matilda were replaced by an armoured operator's cab, housing two Bedford engines to drive the rotor, which carried thirty-nine chains, arranged in three rows. Mine-detonating efficiency was in the order of 90–100 per cent, but the mines tended to damage the chains, and the radius of action was only about 440 yards before the chains were unserviceable. However, the device could successfully cut through two German *Dannert* wire fences, and dig a 12-foot wide path through an earth bank in six minutes. An order for sixty flails was placed with Curran Brothers in January 1943, and the first production vehicle underwent acceptance trials in May 1943.

Meanwhile, a simpler flail device had been developed in the Middle East during 1942. Dubbed the Scorpion, it was mounted on both Matilda II and the M3 Lee/Grant vehicles, although in the former case the main gun was removed. The rotor was carried about four feet above the ground and some seven feet ahead of the tank, with steel rope flails operating at about 115rpm. Unfortunately, the device was mechanically unreliable and was also too wide for the doors of a landing craft. Nevertheless, it was felt to be promising and, in March 1943, twenty-five Scorpion flail sets were ordered for delivery by the end of May. A production prototype was attached to a Valentine, but the trials were far from satisfactory and the device was destroyed by a mine exploding under its belly. Further production was halted pending work on a second prototype which incorporated additional belly protection and on which the flails, now of cable chain, rotated in the opposite direction. On two occasions mines were thrown onto the driver's visor; to counter this, wire netting was fitted to the cross framework. By the end of July 1943, the Scorpion was issued for user trials, but it was eventually abandoned. A proposed 'perambulator' Scorpion was constructed and trialled, but performed so poorly that further development was similarly abandoned, as was work on the Matilda-based Baron and the Sherman-based Marquis.

By the middle of June 1943, there had been sufficient progress with mounting a modified version of the Scorpion flail on a Sherman tank – known as the Crab – and this became the most successful of the flails. Developed by AEC following the unsuccessful trials of the Scorpion 'pram', the Crab differed from other such devices by using the engine of the tank – in this case the Chrysler multi-bank engine of the Sherman V – to drive the flail. The first Crab was inspected in August 1943, with an order for six prototypes rapidly following. One of these was built by AEC, the other five were constructed by T. C. Jones, and in September 1943 the first prototype was ready for trials. The flails were attached to a drum carried six feet ahead of the tank at a constant 51in above the ground; forty-three flails were arranged on the drum in seven spiral rows. With the tank in first gear the drum rotated at 184rpm, giving a mine-detonating efficiency of 91 per cent. An auxiliary gearbox was later used to allow the engine power to be better matched to the flailing speed. Following trials, the design was 'frozen' and work started on the first production vehicle, which included a hydraulic system for raising and lowering the drum.

User trials started at the end of October 1943 and the system proved effective at destroying mines and cutting barbed wire. The hydraulic system allowed the flail to rise at each detonation but, nevertheless, approximately twenty-five chain links were lost each time a mine was detonated and the chains needed to be replaced after seven or eight mines. In fact, the drum was so damaged after detonating twenty-seven German *Tellermines* that it needed to be returned to AEC for repair; nevertheless, work started immediately on building 300 Crabs, for completion by the end of March 1944.

Trials were subsequently conducted with a Crab flail incorporating a Baron rotor and flail layout. Known by the code name Lobster, this project was abandoned in June 1944.

In use, flail tanks were operated in echelon, each vehicle slightly overlapping the path of its predecessor. No practical solution was found to the problems of forward visibility when flailing and a direction gyro and binnacle compass system was fitted to the lead tank, coupled with a speed and distance indicator; battery-operated marker lights were dropped from chutes on the rear tank(s) in the echelon to indicate the cleared area. In April 1944, this system was replaced by the Whyman lane marker, which used flagged stakes fired into the ground by ballistic cartridges.

Ploughs

The first plough for anti-tank mines, developed by John Fowler & Company, was fitted experimentally to a Dragon medium Mk IIIC gun tractor. Consisting of a frame pushed ahead of the vehicle to which were fitted five coulter plough blades in a V arrangement, it was sufficiently successful that, by 1939, it had been adapted to suit the infantry tank Mk I.

In April 1943, Samuel Butler of Leeds developed this idea further to produce the Farmer Front device, which was fitted to a Churchill tank. The number of plough blades was increased to nineteen, arranged in an arrow formation, but the frame was insufficiently strong and tended to buckle in use, leading to the trials being abandoned. The subsequent Farmer Track was also abandoned. The Ipswich-based agricultural engineers, Ransomes, Sims & Jeffries, took the idea a stage further with the Farmer Deck, in which there were two large plough blades together with skids or rollers to provide additional support. Despite a series of promising trials, and a production run of 200, the idea was abandoned in 1944.

Other types of plough were developed and tested by the 79th Armoured Division, with the most successful known as the Bullshorn, but, again, all were eventually abandoned in favour of the flail.

Rollers

Anti-mine rollers had already been developed in the years immediately following the First World War and, in 1937, John Fowler & Company had trialled such a device on a Dragon medium Mk III gun tractor. Described as the anti-mine roller attachment (AMRA) — consisting of a girder frame projecting ahead of the tank carrying four heavy rollers — variants of this device were developed for use with cruiser tank Mks I to IV, the Matilda, Valentine, Covenanter, Crusader and Churchill. This idea was also adapted for the anti-mine reconnaissance castor roller (AMRCR), which proved useful against anti-personnel mines although, like all of the roller devices, it was subsequently superseded by the flails.

Rollers with projecting spikes were tested experimentally in the Middle East. One such device, dubbed Porcupine, was tested in Britain in conjunction with a Sherman, but it was destroyed after dealing with just two German *Tellermines*. The Humber Motor Company proposed a device that used a huge single roller, ten feet in diameter and twelve feet wide, driven by an integral electric motor and designed to be towed behind a tank. The colossal weight of the roller, which was known as Katok, consigned this idea to the scrap heap.

The most successful roller device was devised by General Worthington, Commander of the 4th Canadian Division. In June 1943, he proposed using resiliently mounted heavy rollers on an infantry tank and, by October 1943, a prototype of the Canadian indestructible roller device (CIRD) had been constructed at the Canadian Army workshops at Borden, Hampshire. In conjunction with the Obstacle Assault Centre at Aldershot, the device was attached to a Churchill infantry tank. Following a series of trials, the CIRD was deemed to be sufficiently promising to warrant further investigation and possible production and, in December, arrangements were made to fit the device to a Sherman.

Design parentage was vested in the Deputy Director, Fighting Vehicles (DDFV), with the main contractors being Edwin Danks, a boiler-making company based in Oldbury, Birmingham, Henry Simon of Cheadle Heath, and C. & W. Walker, gas engineers of Donnington, Shropshire. The first production device was trialled in April 1944, and the designs for both Churchill and Sherman tanks were standardised in May 1945. The CIRD consisted of two huge rollers of solid forged armour-quality steel, 16in wide and 26in in diameter, each weighing one ton. The rollers were carried on long arms, arranged to pivot about eight feet ahead of the tank in front of each track, and were suspended on a substantial cross-shaft, with helical springs provided to position the trailing arms.

Curiously, the device appeared to have little effect on the manoeuvrability of the tank; however, unlike the flail, which cleared a broad path, the CIRD cleared mines only in the tracks of the tank — in order to clear a wide path it was necessary to run a number of tanks in a staggered line abreast. One major advantage that the CIRD had over other devices was that there were no mechanical moving parts and thus no need for a vulnerable drive system. It could also be quickly attached to any suitable tank — in the field, if necessary — and similarly jettisoned without too much difficulty. Perhaps most importantly, the fighting abilities of the tank remained unimpaired.

As the trials proceeded, it became apparent that repeated detonations caused the edges of the rollers to spread and to jam in the saddle so that they could not rotate. This was overcome by reducing the width of the rollers by half an inch. Other defects included drooping of the side arms and a tendency for the rollers to seize on the axles. The average life of a roller was seven detonations (of a British Mk IV mine). In an effort to overcome some of the shortcomings, the diameter of the rollers was increased to 28in, and the width to 18in, whilst still maintaining the side clearance, resulting in each of these enlarged rollers now weighing 3,000lb – unfortunately, the increase in weight was too much for the Sherman and the hull bracket attachments failed.

The Churchill proved itself to be made of sterner stuff and, with the improved device fitted the mine-detonating efficiency was increased to 93 per cent and 71 per cent for mines at depths of two inches and four inches respectively. It required 19 detonations in succession of the German *Tellermine* 42 to split one of the larger rollers. Subsequent rollers were able to withstand the detonation of 20 double British Mk IV mines, and one actually withstood the successive detonation of double, triple and quadruple *Tellermine* 42s. There were unsuccessful trials in late 1944 with laminated rollers, consisting of alternate layers of either copper and steel, or rubber and steel, and both were eventually abandoned.

By November 1944, the Sherman-mounted device had also been satisfactorily redesigned to permit the use of 18-inch wide rollers with new side arms. At the same time, design parentage was passed to Edwin Danks. Trials with an even heavier, 21-inch-wide roller showed that there was little to be gained by further increases in size or weight, but a new type of attachment for the trailing arms and the cross-shaft was developed which reduced the amount by which the roller could wander on the shaft.

In May 1944, the CIRD was also adapted for use with the Cromwell and Comet tanks. Changes were made to the shape and method of attachment of the side arms to allow them to be fixed to the front of the hull, reducing the overall mine-detonating efficiency to 77 per cent. The device was passed to the Assault Training and Development Centre in June 1944 for user trials but, not long after this, the War Office concluded that land mines were not presenting a particular problem and the project was cancelled.

Rollers continued to be used for mine clearance, with devices such as Rodent, Lulu and Centipede used with some degree of success. The Lulu system was particularly interesting since the device attempted to adapt the successful Polish electro-magnetic mine-detection system for use with a tank.

Tank 'Dozers

Redundant Valentine, Matilda, Crusader, Alecto and Centaur tanks were all converted to the 'dozer role, generally by removing the turret and fitting a structure to the sides of the hull which could support a steel bulldozer blade. The blade was raised and lowered by a winch in the fighting compartment using a cable running over a tripod structure at the front of the hull. The Churchill AVRE could also be fitted with a 'dozer blade. Of these, only the Matilda and the Churchill AVRE retained the main gun.

These tanks proved themselves to be invaluable in clearing streets of the rubble of shelled buildings during the advance across Europe.

In May 1940, in an attempt to counter German massed air strikes in France, the British Army hastily adapted the Vickers Mk V light tank for the anti-aircraft role, typically fitting two or four 15mm Besa machine guns in a special turret. *(Warehouse Collection)*

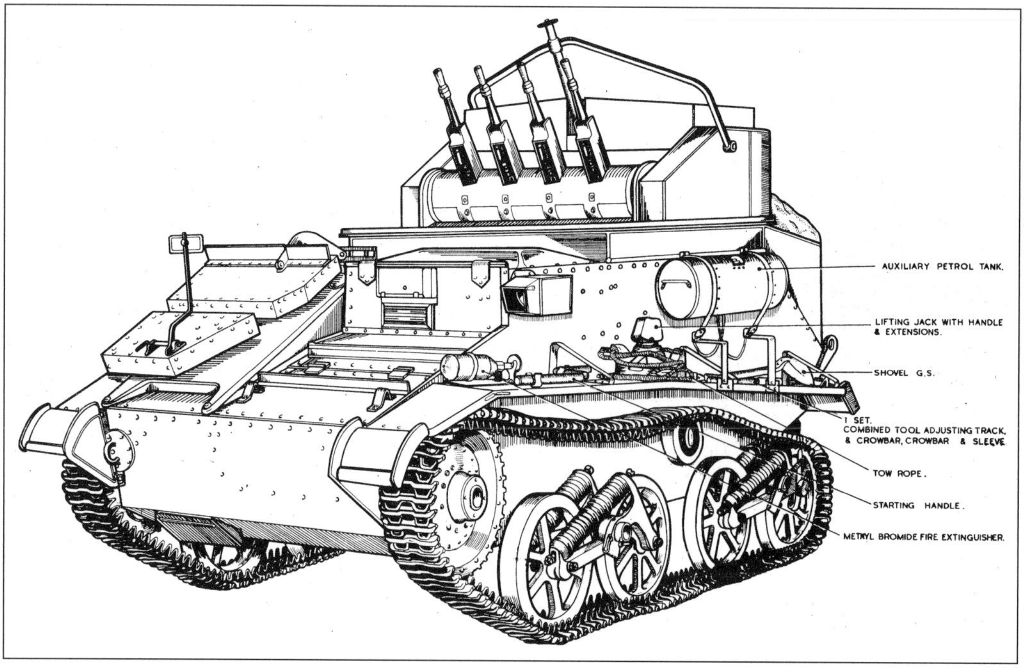
AUXILIARY PETROL TANK.
LIFTING JACK WITH HANDLE & EXTENSIONS.
SHOVEL G.S.
1 SET. COMBINED TOOL ADJUSTING TRACK, & CROWBAR, CROWBAR & SLEEVE.
TOW ROPE.
STARTING HANDLE.
METHYL BROMIDE FIRE EXTINGUISHER.

Exterior stowage diagram for the light anti-aircraft tank. *(Warehouse Collection)*

Crusader II equipped for the anti-aircraft role. *(Warehouse Collection)*

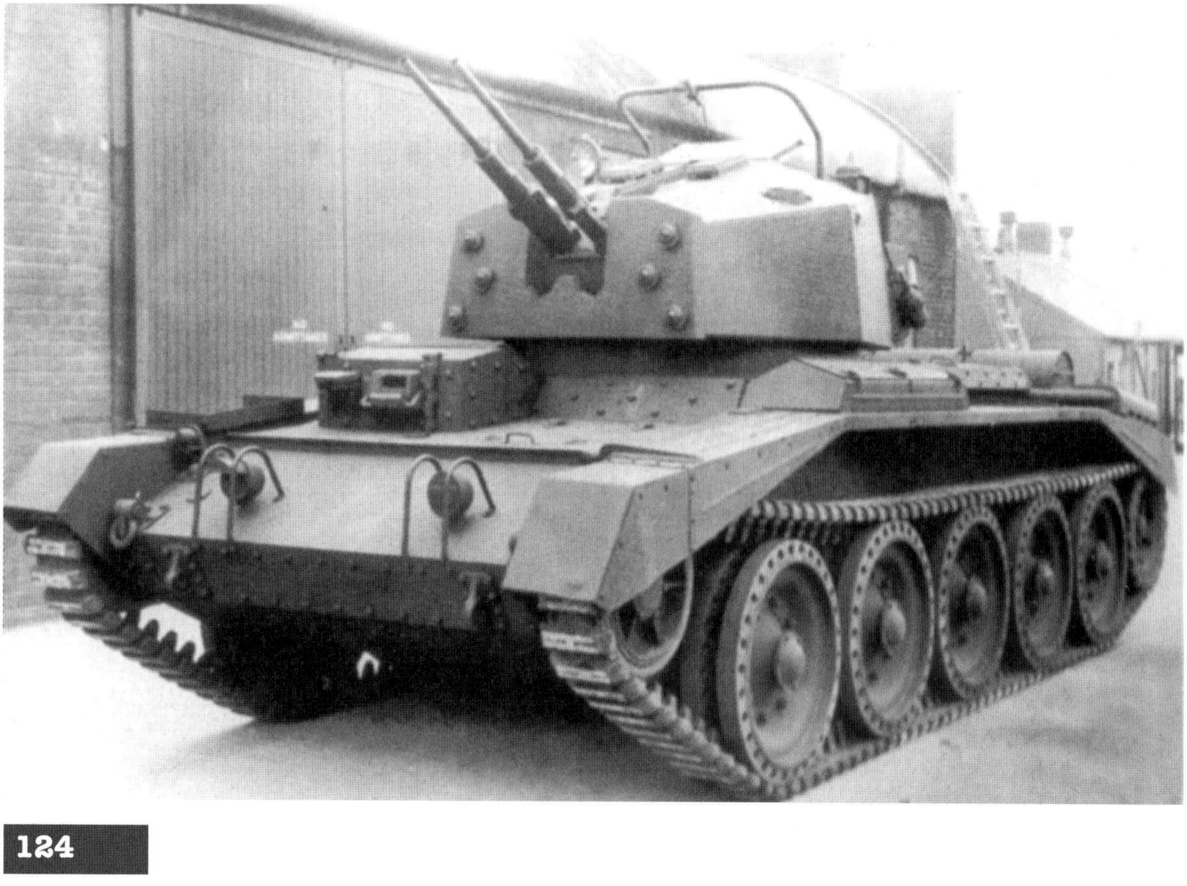

In the Churchill ARV Mk I, seen here towing a Churchill II on a tracked trailer, the turret opening was covered by a roof plate that included escape hatches, and twin Bren guns were provided for anti-aircraft defence. *(Tank Museum)*

Designed by REME workshops, the Churchill ARV Mk II was fitted with a fixed turret, mounting a dummy gun and housing a Croft 60-ton winch. *(Tank Museum)*

Similar to the Churchill-based ARV Mk II, the Sherman version had a dummy gun and was fitted with a 60-ton winch. *(Warehouse Collection)*

Photographed at the REME Museum, this M32B1 Sherman ARV is based on the cast-hull of the M4A1. *(Warehouse Collection)*

On the Sherman BARV, the engine air inlet and exhaust outlets were raised above the waterline, and a substantial timber pusher pad was attached to the nose. The BARV was very successful during the landing stages of the invasion of Europe in 1944. *(IWM, B5578)*

This privately owned Sherman BARV was recovered from a Portsmouth scrapyard and painstakingly restored. *(Simon Thomson)*

The Churchill AVRE was fitted with a 290mm *Pétard* spigot mortar. *(Tank Museum)*

The Churchill AVRE remained in service into the post-war years. This version was photographed in 1949. *(Warehouse Collection)*

Churchill AVRE with the Bobbin Carpet Mk II canvas mat. *(Warehouse Collection)*

On the Covenanter bridgelayer, the turret was removed and the scissor bridge was carried across the hull in a folded position ready to be launched from the nose. *(Warehouse Collection)*

When the folded sections of the Covenanter bridge reached the vertical position, the two components began to separate, opening out to the full width; once the bridge sections were horizontal, they could be laid across the gap and the tank could be disengaged. *(Tank Museum)*

The Covenanter bridgelayer lacked reliability and tended to be reserved for training, but the Valentine saw some service in north-west Europe following the D-Day landings. *(Warehouse Collection)*

Valentine bridgelayer with the bridge in the travelling position. *(Warehouse Collection)*

Churchill bridgelayer with the bridge laid across the hull for travelling. *(Warehouse Collection)*

Archer self-propelled gun demonstrating the Churchill 30-foot bridge (bridge, tank, 30ft, no 2).
(*Warehouse Collection*)

Churchill Ark Mk II, Italian pattern. In this design, there were no trackways across the hull itself.
(*Warehouse Collection*)

Although it never got beyond the prototype stage, the Churchill Great Eastern was a more sophisticated development of the ramp carrier with a span of 60 feet; rocket power was used to launch the ramp sections across the opening. *(Warehouse Collection)*

The Churchill Lakeman Ark had trackways elevated above the turret, with a ramp at the rear. *(Warehouse Collection)*

Valentine DD with the wading screen in the collapsed position. Three prototypes were constructed by July 1942, and Metropolitan-Cammell was commissioned to start to convert 450 Valentine V, IX and XI variants. The number was later increased to 625. *(Simon Thomson)*

Preserved Valentine DD tank with the wading screen erected. Although the canvas screen prevented the driver from seeing where he was going, thus making the commander's role indispensable, once ashore, it could be quickly lowered and the tank could assume its fighting role. The Valentine could only swim with the turret traversed to the rear. *(Simon Thomson)*

Most DD tanks were constructed using the Sherman hull. The Sherman was readily available and, perhaps most importantly, the position of the turret allowed the tank to swim with its gun forward which meant that it was ready to fire as soon as land was reached and the screen was collapsed. *(IWM, B5897)*

Sherman DD photographed in the water with the wading screen erected. The screens were manufactured by the Firestone Tyre Company. *(Warehouse Collection)*

Churchill Crocodile in action – there is little doubt that the flame-thrower inspired a greater dread on the part of those that came into contact with it than any other weapon. A captured German general told British interrogators that 'of all the weapons at your disposal, my men most feared your flame-throwers.' (Warehouse Collection)

Churchill Crocodile showing the gas-pressurised two-wheeled trailer, which carried 400 gallons of petroleum-based fuel. The trailer could be jettisoned once the fuel had been consumed. (Warehouse Collection)

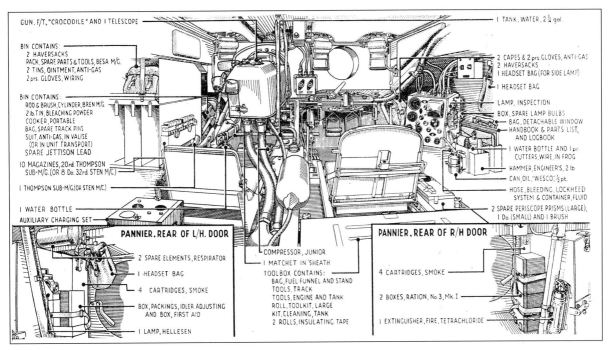

GUN, F/T, "CROCODILE" AND I TELESCOPE

I TANK, WATER, 2¾ gal

BIN CONTAINS:—
2 HAVERSACKS
PACK, SPARE PARTS & TOOLS, BESA M/G.
2 TINS, OINTMENT, ANTI-GAS
2 prs. GLOVES, WIRING

BIN CONTAINS:—
ROD & BRUSH, CYLINDER, BREN M/G.
2 lb. TIN, BLEACHING POWDER
COOKER, PORTABLE
BAG, SPARE TRACK PINS
SUIT, ANTI-GAS, IN VALISE
(OR IN UNIT TRANSPORT)
SPARE JETTISON LEAD

10 MAGAZINES, 20 rd. THOMPSON
SUB-M/G. (OR 8 Do. 32 rd. STEN M/C.)

I THOMPSON SUB-M/G. (OR STEN M/C.)

I WATER BOTTLE

AUXILIARY CHARGING SET

2 CAPES & 2 prs. GLOVES, ANTI-GAS
2 HAVERSACKS
I HEADSET BAG (FOR SIDE LAMP)
I HEADSET BAG

LAMP, INSPECTION
BOX, SPARE LAMP BULBS
BAG, DETACHABLE WINDOW
HANDBOOK & PARTS LIST,
AND LOGBOOK
I WATER BOTTLE AND I pr.
CUTTERS, WIRE, IN FROG
HAMMER, ENGINEER'S, 2 lb
CAN, OIL, "WESCO", ½ pt.
HOSE, BLEEDING, LOCKHEED
SYSTEM & CONTAINER, FLUID
2 SPARE PERISCOPE PRISMS (LARGE),
I Do. (SMALL) AND I BRUSH

PANNIER, REAR OF L/H. DOOR

2 SPARE ELEMENTS, RESPIRATOR
I HEADSET BAG
4 CARTRIDGES, SMOKE
BOX, PACKINGS, IDLER ADJUSTING
AND BOX, FIRST AID
I LAMP, HELLESEN

COMPRESSOR, JUNIOR
I MATCHET IN SHEATH

TOOLBOX CONTAINS:—
BAG, FUEL FUNNEL AND STAND
TOOLS, TRACK
TOOLS, ENGINE AND TANK
ROLL, TOOLKIT, LARGE
KIT, CLEANING, TANK
2 ROLLS, INSULATING TAPE

PANNIER, REAR OF R/H. DOOR

4 CARTRIDGES, SMOKE
2 BOXES, RATION, No. 3, Mk. I
I EXTINGUISHER, FIRE, TETRACHLORIDE

Driver's compartment stowage diagram for the Churchill Crocodile. *(Warehouse Collection)*

The first production mine flails, known as the Scorpion, were attached to the Valentine III, but were abandoned following user trials. *(Warehouse Collection)*

When the Octopus flail was attached to the Sherman it became known as the Marquis, but it was eventually abandoned in favour of the Crab. *(Warehouse Collection)*

By the middle of June 1943, a modified version of the Scorpion flail had been mounted on a Sherman tank. Known as the Crab, the tank retained both turret and gun, and the Crab became the most successful of the flails. *(Warehouse Collection)*

German prisoners of war stand knee-deep in the sea watching a Jeep being towed ashore. Behind them is a Sherman Crab belonging to the Westminster Dragoons. *(IWM, B5089)*

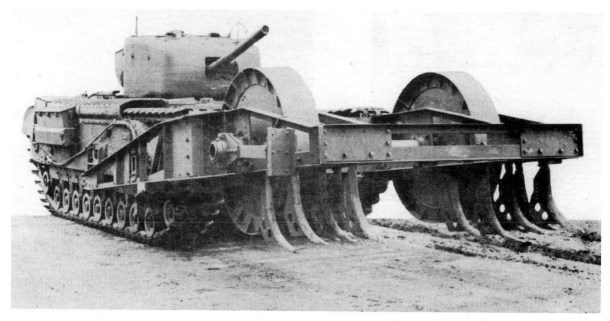

Developed by Samuel Butler, the Farmer Track plough used a pair of five-foot-diameter wheels to support the six spring tines which were intended to lift the buried mines. The device became clogged in use and further development was abandoned in December 1943. *(Warehouse Collection)*

The CIRD was designed to be driven through an area believed to contain mines, where pressure from the heavy roller would detonate any mines immediately under the roller. Mine-detonating efficiency was 83 per cent for mines laid at a depth of two inches, reducing to 65 per cent when the depth was increased to four inches. The device was used in conjunction with Cromwell, Comet and Sherman (*seen here*) tanks. *(Warehouse Collection)*

The upward blast from an exploding mine caused the roller of the CIRD, and its trailing arm, to rotate around the cross-shaft and come to rest upside down, with a spade on the cross-shaft digging into the ground. As the tank moved forward, the spade would cause the roller and its trailing arm to return to its normal position. *(Warehouse Collection)*

The Polish-designed Lulu detector mechanism used non-metallic rollers on arms positioned ahead of the vehicle. When the roller passed over a mine, or a similar piece of metal, the electrical balance between two coils was disturbed and a signal was sent to the vehicle. Prototypes were built but it was never tried in combat. *(Warehouse Collection)*

The Centaur 'dozer tank was converted by Foden from the standard gun tank and was allocated to regiments equipped with the Cromwell. *(Warehouse Collection)*